D0791925

PUNCH AFLOAT

PUNCH AFLOAT

Edited by **WILLIAM DAVIS**

DAVID & CHARLES
NEWTON ABBOT LONDON NORTH PROMFRET (VT)
VANCOUVER

ISBN O 7153 6843 5

Set in 10 on 11pt Times New Roman and printed in
Great Britain by The Leagrave Press Ltd., Luton and London
for David & Charles (Holdings) Limited
South Devon House Newton Abbot Devon

Published in the United States of America
by David & Charles Inc
North Pomfret Vermont 05053 USA

Published in Canada
by Douglas David & Charles Limited
3645 McKechnie Drive West Vancouver BC

CONTENTS

Introduction

I ADORE yachts. Big, fast, expensive yachts. They are my one luxury, my one indulgence. You can mess about in boats if you like; I'd rather mess about in staterooms. There is only one laughably small stipulation, a mere detail. *They must belong to someone else.*

If ocean racing is, as someone once said, "like standing under a cold shower tearing up five pound notes" then running a luxury yacht must be like throwing them overboard in sackfuls. It takes all the fun out of being afloat. I much prefer to leave sordid commercial considerations to other people, preferably multi-millionaires. Yachts, real yachts, are built to accommodate at least a dozen passengers. Which leaves their owners with the problem of finding enough guests to share their trip. You think it's easy? You'd be surprised how much trouble it can be. All your fellow millionaires will naturally be on their own yachts, or at their villas in the South of France. Other business friends will be too busy trying to become millionaires to have time for holidays. And employees are ruled out because it's bad policy to mix socially with one's underlings. It might give them dangerous ideas and, besides, there is no point in impressing *them*.

Which is where you and I come in. The basic qualifications needed in a guest are few: a sizeable capacity for drink, a stomach that doesn't mind being tossed about a bit, an adequate stock of small talk, and a total lack of interest in whatever happens on the bridge or in the wheel house. (If there is one thing every owner dislikes it's being upstaged by some smart know-all, even if he *has* spent twenty years in the Navy). It also helps to have a title or, failing that, to be an accomplished name-dropper. I know one Italian aristocrat who is swamped with invitations every year because he once knew the Duke of Windsor. You will naturally be expected to hate Socialists; much of the conversation on board will centre around the shocking state of business confidence and the lack of fiscal incentive. (One of my fondest memories is of a cruise on the luxury yacht of a Greek shipping tycoon. We drank gallons of *Dom Perignom* at breakfast and nibbled whitebait served by white-jacketed flunkeys. At noon we switched to caviar and *Chateau Lafite*. While we were eating we discussed business. My host seemed deeply depressed and I succeeded in making them more gloomy still; the world, we agreed, was in a frightful mess).

Poor sailors are advised to settle for one of those yachts which never move out of the harbour. Well, hardly ever. At the height of the season the harbour at Cannes and other fashionable watering places is packed with floating cocktail parties. The host might make an occasional foray to St. Tropez, but in the main he will be content to stay where guests are plentiful and everyone can admire his expensive status symbol. There is also, of course, the other kind. This one is constantly on the move and will take you to islands you have never heard of. Islands where you can swim or water-ski in water of unbelievable clarity; islands whose beaches are gloriously empty; islands with magnificent vegetation and hospitable natives. But check, before you go, whether you are expected to do any work. Some people love to scrub decks, hoist sails or whatever and it may well be exactly what you had in mind when you accepted. It can certainly be fun. But it obviously pays to find out about these things beforehand; you may have been invited simply because he couldn't get a professional crew or because he is too mean to hire one.

I have a weakness for islands myself and love to be at sea. I like to think that I can handle a cocktail glass as well as the next man but I prefer to be out and about, away from the multitude. My last ten summer holidays have been spent in the Aeolian islands, off Sicily. My base is a small house on Lipari, but most of the days are spent afloat. There is no shortage of yachts in the harbour and I gladly accept offers to visit one of the other six islands—in part, I confess, because it gives me pleasure to show newcomers around. But I am just as happy exploring quiet little bays in a modest sailing boat. And once you know the ropes, the thrill of cutting across a body of water at full tilt can compare to racing a Ferrari at 150. (Given today's speed limits on crowded roads it's also a lot easier and safer). My most memorable trip was not on a yacht but a fishing boat, going after *pesce spada*, Swordfish. Twelve meters long, it was equipped with a 25 meter high mast from which the lookout did the steering. The harpoonist lay at the tip of a 35 meter long extension and the Boat was packed with empty oil drums—to be thrown into the water when we made a hit, so that the *pesce spada* could exhaust himself dragging it around. I can't say I envied the two professionals but I loved the thrill of the chase and shared their excitement when we made a handsome catch.

My own boat, the only one I have ever owned, is really not much more than a dinghy with an outboard motor. There is no sun-deck (hell, the whole thing *is* the sun-deck) and I drink my cocktails out of a thermos flask. But it gets me to all sorts of places which are inacessible to larger craft, and it allows me to fish and skin-dive. From time to time we go out at night, equipped with a lantern, to fish for *calamari* and cook it on some small beach. It may not be the high life, but I dare say I have more fun than a lot of multi-millionaires. And this, of course, is the whole point of life afloat. Even the most sumptuous yacht can be a let-down if you lack the capacity for enjoyment—if, instead of welcoming the many delights it can offer, you spend your days fretting about business contracts and wondering whether they can manage without you at the office.

This book is for all boating enthusiasts. Punch has been publishing articles and cartoons about life afloat for more than a century and we felt it was time that some were put between hard covers. I have included contributions from the past as well as the present so that you can make your own comparison. I have also added some articles about fishing because, for many people, boating and fishing are inseparable. I sincerely hope the book will add to your pleasure.

WILLIAM DAVIS

"*And even if we do get back, I bet all the moorings are taken.*"

Harry Secombe and the Sea

The big game fisherman extraordinary sends word from the Caribbean

I HAVE always been fascinated by fish, with or without chips. A lot of my time as a schoolboy in Swansea was spent watching the trawlers unloading their glittering catches at the dockside; the slabs of fishmongers' shops draw me like a magnet; Jacques Cousteau on television is an irresistible attraction, and I even bought the house in which I am now living because it had the largest tropical fish tank in South London. Unfortunately it was in the room where I rehearse my singing and an aria or two used to send the Angel Fish leaping out of the water. Eventually I gave the fish away on humanitarian grounds, with the exception of an apparently deaf Catfish which died of natural causes during a cold spell.

It is small wonder then that when my horizons began to open up I was eager to emulate Hemingway's "Old Man and the Sea". I could see the big fish jumping high in the air, shaking the hook from side to side in a frantic effort to get free, whilst I sat firmly strapped in my chair hauling it inexorably towards the waiting gaff, exultant in victory and yet sad for the death of a brave adversary. "Vaya con Dios" I would say, patting the dying fish.

But all my real-life experiences have never been like that. I have fished the waters of the Caribbean, the Coral Sea and the South Pacific, yet as a big game fisherman I am somewhere near the bottom of the fourth division and due for imminent relegation. In Acapulco—where the Sailfish and Black Marlin are of legendary size and everybody who goes out fishing comes back with something to show for it—when it came to my turn to take the chair I was being sick over the side. Something extremely large and vicious once took bait, hook, line and rod from me when fishing off Montego Bay. It was either a shark or a Russian submarine. I once went fishing with an eccentric retired army officer on the Great Barrier Reef. We had been out six hours without success when he shouted "Strike!" as the line screamed away. He pushed me into the chair and I began hauling away frantically, my heart pounding and the Foster's lager burning in my throat.

"It's a Marlin," he said, jumping up and down and making the boat rock from side to side. I reeled in grimly.

I made one last desperate haul on the rod and up came the hook and away went a permanently smiling Marlin. My companion threw down the gaff, saying nothing as he went forward to start the engine. We made a U turn and headed back for the mainland at full speed, the lines streaming out behind us with the baited hooks a foot above our wake.

"What are we after now?" I asked lamely.

"Bloody Flying Fish," he said without looking round.

My most recent fishing expedition was off Barbados last Christmas when I thought it prudent to do a little research for this article, having imprudently accepted the commission. We were staying, my family and I, at a hotel on that little gem of an island, and I hired a boat big enough to take us all. At eight o'clock I mustered my wife and progeny on the beach to await the launch. We had only been standing there long enough for my six-year-old daughter, Katy, to throw my eleven-year-old son David's book of horror stories into the sea to be rescued by her fifty-two-year-old father, when my twenty-four-year-old daughter, Jennifer, and my twenty-year-old son, Andrew, both pointed out to sea at a fast approaching cabin cruiser of surprising elegance and size. "That's nice," remarked Myra, my fortyish wife.

A smart dinghy buzzed towards the beach piloted by a natty gent who stepped nimbly ashore and approached our suitably impressed group.

"Mrs. Goldsmith's party?" he enquired.

"Over here!" cried a large American lady wearing yachting gear from behind us.

"Oh!" we said collectively, and Katy threw David's book into the water again.

Eventually we found ourselves aboard a smaller and less elegant fishing boat, but one which was fully equipped for the job. The skipper, a jolly person of a build not unlike my own, made us welcome as we headed for the deep blue water beyond the reef. We arranged ourselves around the boat—my wife and Jennifer found places in which to tan themselves, Katy and David sat in the fishing chairs and Andrew and I sat on the stern looking for any sudden flurry of flying fish, a sure sign of big fish in the area.

"This is the life," I said removing my shirt and sun hat.

"You'll get burnt again," said Myra.

"Nonsense," I said, "I've taken two sunburn prevention tablets."

She lay back again. "We'll see," she said.

We trolled our lines for an hour, following the coastline.

"How about a drink?" said the skipper.

"Too early," said Myra, knowing me.

"It may be half past nine here, but it's half past one in London," I laughed.

Soon Andy, Jennifer and I were drinking our rum and cokes while Myra and the kids contented themselves with lemonade.

"What fish might we catch?" I asked the captain.

"Spanish Mackerel, perhaps, Wahoo or Kingfish, Barracuda, Dolphin . . ."

Katy sat up. "You're not going to catch a Dolphin," she cried. "They're lovely. Flipper's a Dolphin."

David looked up from his sodden book.

"The Dolphin is an active pelagic spiny-finned fish constituting a genus coryphaena," he quoted accurately. "Flipper is a Porpoise."

"No he's not!" yelled Katy and threw his book into the sea for the last time.

"I'd finished it anyway," he said sticking out his tongue.

This isn't Hemingway, I thought, it's A.A. Milne.

Time passed quickly enough with the rum and coke flowing freely, and after I had conducted the family choir in "The Lord's My Shepherd" for the fourth time, with Jennifer getting gradually weaker on the descant, I got up to make my third trip to the tiny toilet.

"You'll be sorry," said Myra squinting up at me as I passed her. I laughed indulgently.

" . . . and **I** *could cut down palm trees and make us a cosy hut, and* **you** *could gather wild fruit and milk the goats . . . "*

I had just locked myself in the loo when I heard "STRIKE!" from the captain and confused shouts and screams from the others. I tried to open the bolt on the door and snagged my thumb rather badly. Katy banged on the door screaming "Andy's killing Flipper!" I banged back shouting "I can't get out. Tell your mother!" By the time I had forced the door, leaking blood from my thumb as I did so, it was all over and Andrew had landed a 35-pound Wahoo—modest enough for these waters, but still bigger than anything I had ever managed to catch. We had drinks all round again and the boat circled looking for another victim. It never came, and when we landed later with the catch I stood in the background nursing my injured thumb as Andy posed with the Wahoo.

That night Myra had to send for the doctor. "What's wrong with him?" he asked as he came in.

"Rum, sun and thumb," she said. "And a touch of the Hemingways."

THE FIRST BOAT

GRAHAM's maiden voyage

"Have you the same thing in a smaller size?"

"If we have to sell the car to pay for it, how do we get it to the Grand Union Canal?"

"Oh boy! Stainless steel chain plate . . .backstay anchorage, Stemhead roller with Continental fairleads, forward mooring alloy cleat, adjustable jib fairleads, centre mainsheet traveller, teak rubbing strakes . . ."

"Considering it was our first lock, I think we did very well."

"When I say 'Now', lasso that tree stump!"

"Can you slow up for a minute? I'm trying to cut my toe-nails."

"Arthur says she can **do up** *to thirty knots . . . whatever they are."*

"Shore ahoy! Are we all right for Stratford?"

"Every year the same. After the regatta you'll cool off and go back to that skinny Linda Rawlings."

Glossary of Sailing

Sailing terms are easy to remember as long as you realise that sailors never call anything by the obvious name. Sailing itself is dead simple; picking up the language takes a little longer.

ABAFT, ATHWART Meaningless swear words.

ABEAM A big plank.

AHEAD A tiny lavatory.

ANTLE A small windstay attached to the port lug with a catscrew which can be adjusted by a righandle to bring the mainsail crashing down.

BACK & FRONT It would be sensible to call the back and front of the boat the back and front of the boat, so they don't. The front is actually the beginning of a new weather system. It would be sensible to call the end of an old weather system a back, so they don't. Aback is actually a sail with its clew sheeted to windward, Whatever that means.

BAIL "For God's sake do you want us all to drown don't just sit there like a stuffed dummy but get some of that water out of here!". This is called asking for bail.

BACKSTAY Time allowed in port between races.

BINNACLE Sort of mechanical device with which many boats get encrusted, making progress through the water difficult.

BLOCK Crew member.

BURGEE A small Australian cage bird.

BOOM A loud noise to mark the start of the race; traditionally the point at which you find yourself tacking the wrong way on the wrong side of the line.

CLEAT A short, sharp, agonising blow on the elbow from a metal protuberance.

CLEW Chinese crew.

GYBE To make fun of a crew member after he has e.g. fallen overboard.

HULL Well-known seaport.

HOVE TO So is Hove.

JURY RIGGING Illegally fixing the result of a race.

KNOT Unit of distance; the distance travelled during the time it takes to tie a knot.

LEEWARD Pronounced 'looard', this means the direction of the nearest lavatory.

LOG Large, semi-submerged book in which the voyage is charted, and which can cause a nastly hole in the hull.

PILKER A small bluff attached to the lansail stick through which runs a stay-yard which can be used to control the jibrun.

ROPE Rope, of course, is never, never called rope. Ropes are called stays or guys or

sheets or halyards or warps or lanyards or bridles or shrouds—call them anything you like, in fact, *but don't call them ropes.*

SHEET Obviously, this is word for a sail. So you won't be surprised to learn it means a rope.

SPAT A friendly fight to decide who shall put up the spinnaker.

SPINNAKER GUY The fellow who loses the fight and puts up the spinnaker.

SPINNAKER BOOM A short-lived upsurge in the selling of spinnakers from 1969 to 1971 which fizzled out suddenly and left many spinnaker makers bankrupt.

SPLICE A highly complicated knot used to join two ends of videotape.

STERN Descriptive of the captain's expression as he watches the crew try to put up the spinnaker.

TACK Lunch (also Bight).

TWINE The name by which Mark Twain is known in Australia.

WHIPPING or LASHING A traditional naval punishment. It consists of making the crew spend hours on end tying up frayed ends of rope.

YAWL A heart greeting (Deep South of America).

BUMS IN BOATS

by James Wentworth Day

"HOW do I get out of here to the sea, Guv?"

He peered at me from the driving seat of a long, grinning American motor-car, tastefully bedizened in sky-blue and silver. A sky-blue and silver boat-trailer was appended to it. Upon it rested, like a nightmare swan, a sky-blue and silver speed boat. The lot was jammed in a narrow Essex lane. Below, at the foot of the field, cloud-topped elms marched to the blue of the Blackwater Estuary. Gulls made snowflakes against a high blue sky. The cuckoo jeered derisively. Reed-warblers twittered in dyke-side reeds. The blue and silver entourage struck a jarring note.

The Jehu of this set-up was long, thin, sallow, with black sideboards and sleek black hair, slicked back. He wore a blue and silver V-necked sweater, white trousers and suede shoes. He reeked of money, whelks and winkles.

"You'll have to back up out of this lane, half a mile or more," I told him. "You can't go beyond the field gates. There's a bull in the field."

"Cor blast!" he ejaculated. "It'll take me a bleedin' half hour to reverse this lot up this alley. I wanter go for a spin on the sea, see?"

"Try Bradwell when you get into the road." I said. "They've got a concrete hard. But look out for mudbanks, the nuclear power station barrage, two sunken barges, scores of mooring buoys, half of them submerged, shell banks and old ships' anchors. This river's got everything, including bits of German aeroplanes."

"When I get her going, Guv," he confided, "she lifts three-quarters of her hull out of the water, sits on her bum and fair roars off. Two thousand nickers' worth."

I left him reversing painfully up the tree-bordered lane. Brambles and buckthorn took their toll of blue and silver paint remorselessly. I did not tell him that Bradwell-juxta-Mare has asked for a ban on high-powered speed boats.

Sea Hogs are the new menace of the coast. They arrive from nowhere, towing their craft and launch them in the glittering sea-silence of a curlew-haunted creek, or amid the yachts, fishing smacks, dinghies, prams, punts, buoys, mooring ropes and submerged anchors of a crowded but innocent fairway. Mersea Quarters, Brightlingsea, Steeple Beach, Burnham-on-Crouch, or pretty well anywhere you like to name on the East and South coasts—all suffer from them.

Once they hit the water all hell breaks loose. A roar from the exhaust. A sudden bow-wave swamps dinghies, turns tanned old gentlemen puce, scares old ladies out of their wits, sends bathers scuttling to safety, sets kids howling, dogs barking and fishermen cursing. They are everybody's enemy and nobody's friend. Some are near-silent. A sibilant hum, that's all. These are the potential villains. Sooner, rather than later, an innocent bather, head barely showing in the trough of a short sea, swimming from an anchored yacht, well out in the fairway, will be beheaded. Then the real row will start.

It could not happen? Can't it? Recently off the hard at Mersea Island, on the Essex coast, a fibre-glass boat roaring through the crowded anchorage, hit a semi-submerged

"Fair's fair—he does all the decorating!"

mooring buoy. It was submerged just about as much as a swimmer's head would have been. The speed-boat promptly split in half. The stern sank like a stone. The bows shot up. Cushioned with air, they floated grotesquely on the tide. Two garish figures in yellow oilskins and gaudy skull-caps, the crew of the horror-boat, clung, precariously to the bobbing wreckage.

"Laugh! I damn near split me trousers," said Bert the oyster-man. "They come floatin' on the tide past my owd dredger a-hollerin', 'Save us! Chuck us a rope!"

"Not bloody likely," I says. 'You damn near swamped my dinghy yesterday. You can swim ashore now. An' I hope the owd crabs make a meal of you.' Lor'! They swum ashore, got on the mud where that's soft, tried to walk, fell down and went up to their arm-pits! I hollered to 'em to roll on their backs. Time they done that they was out of the soft and on the hard mud—an' looking *all* mud! P'raps that'll larn 'em to come on our waters."

Not all speed-boats roar through anchorages but alas, to the average Sea Hog, the sea-silence is there to be shattered by the roar of his engine. He batters the sky with din. The gulls' way becomes the ghouls' way. The opal sheen of mudflats in the sun, the stippled silver of a quiet sea, the wine-red purple of sheets of sea-lavender in bloom, the threnody of wind in rigging, the quiet lap of the tide against an anchored boat, the dipping flight and plummet plunge of terns diving for tiny fish, the aerial fantasy of the wings of wildfowl and seafowl, and the cresting challenge of running white-caps "on the Main" mean nothing to the Sea Hog. He is blind to beauty, bereft of sea-sense. He lives for noise, speed and show-off. The child of the Affluent Society. The Road Hog who has taken to water.

He contributes nothing to local rates, nothing in mooring dues and less to the peace and safety of those who live by the sea and love it. These "bums in boats" are a menace on the Norfolk Broads, a pest on the Essex coast and a curse in the sheltered waters of the Wight, Lymington and other sea-ways of enchantment. Speed limits should be enforced and all offenders prosecuted.

NOT WANTED ON VOYAGE
NOT WANTED ON VOYAGE
NOT WANTED ON VOYAGE
NOT WANTED ON VOYAGE
Sprod

AIR-CONDITIONED, CENTRALLY HEATED, PLUSH LINED SEA FEVER

MAHOOD looks at how the rich mess about in boats

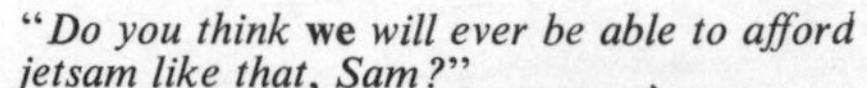

"Do you think **we** *will ever be able to afford jetsam like that, Sam?"*

"Would you check the air conditioning, Tompkins, I think I can smell the sea!"

"Fiona! Get on the radio phone and find out what the pound is standing at!"

"*It must be one of the bloody nouveau riche yachts sinking—those are* **super** *rats!*"

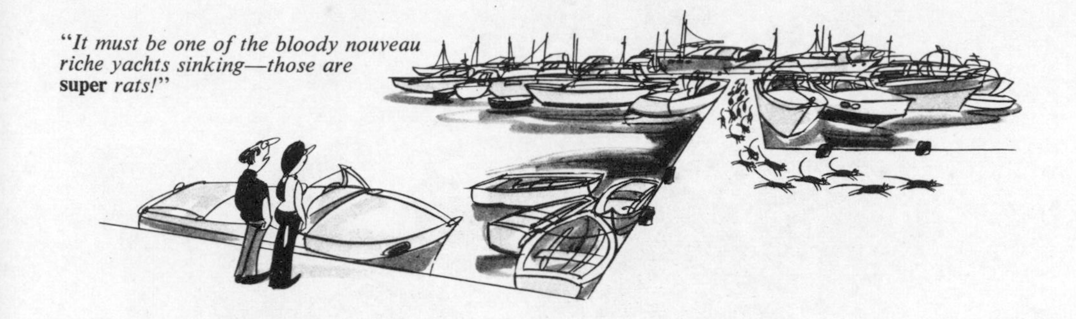

"*There's no need to panic, I think we have all the necessities—the champers, the caviar, the colour TV, the suntan lotion . . .*"

"*That's nothing—we've been burgled off the coasts of France, Italy, Spain, Morocco, Corsica* **and** *Greece!*"

"*Bloody nerve! If it wasn't for the unacceptable face of capitalism he wouldn't have any damn yachts to race against!*"

"I sneaked down to 'Tourist' last night and you wouldn't believe what goes on down there."

Anyone for Tennis?

asks *RICHARD GORDON*

SPORTY-MINDED travellers, intending to spread their pounds as thinly as possible over the earth's surface by taking a cruise, can pack their games kit in confidence that most of their favourite pastimes will be available afloat. The equipment is generally fashioned from traditional nautical furnishings, with the same charming ingenuity as ships' funerals are conducted with canvas and twine, weighty fire-bars, and a well sandpapered hatch cover. *Tennis* can for instance be adapted for any reasonably sized square of deck, using a net made from a cargo-hoist and quoits from tarred rope in canvas jackets. The scoring follows lawn tennis, the rules are simple, and can vary with the whim of the captain. *It should never be attempted by anyone over the age of thirty.*

This warning is needed through the peculiar social structure of life on shipboard, a grasp of which can reduce the risk of physical and mental injury to the gamesplayer.

Going to sea, like going to Heaven, gives everyone a fresh start. The landlubberly past drops as swiftly from memory as the disppearing coastline. Social position ashore becomes meaningless in an autocracy where the captain represents, as occasion demands, the Queen, the Law, and the Established Church. Even clothes carry no distinction, one bikini or pair of shorts much resembling any other. Money is irrelevant, there being nothing to spend it on except gin and haircuts, both of which are very reasonable. A cruise ship is not a means of transport, but a comfortable, well-victualled desert island. Why people will pay heavily to involve themselves in such a primitive society is known only to deep-thinking anthropologists and the advertising executives of shipping lines.

The passengers on a cruise thus face the same situation as so inconvenienced the *Bounty* mutineers on Pitcairn Island. Any females available must be fought for, and the nicer they are the nastier the scrap. Blatant rough-and-tumbles on the boat deck being frowned upon by the authorities, the aggression becomes restricted to the ship's games. I once watched a pair of Tarzans playing the finals of the deck tennis competition, under a blazing sun and the eyes of the sexiest girl aboard, with a ferocity which ended the contest by putting one in the ship's hospital with a suspected fractured ankle, and the other in with a suspected coronary occlusion.

Table-tennis, the rowing machine, the gymnasium fixed bicycle, pillow-fighting on the greasy pole, even bouncing on the trampoline, are similarly abused as primaeval exhibitions of masculine vigour. Even *Walking* is a perilous activity at sea. The knowledge that five times round the promenade deck equals a mile seems to obsess overweight males who ashore wouldn't stroll out to post a letter. Possibly they feel diminished by leaving behind their expensive cars and other status symbols of a bulkier nature, seeking to raise themselves in the eyes of the near-naked female sunbathers with a spectacle of physical endurance. Even in the tropics these salt-water hikers puff round amazing distances, calling loudly at each circuit how they would have progressed from Hyde Park Corner to Woking, and finally collapsing outside Basingstoke.

There are fortunately more peaceful sports aboard for passengers in whom the primitive urge to mate burns less fiercely. Bowls is the game probably most free of sexual undertones. Even in beautifully stabilised ships this pastime must be adapted as *Shuffleboard*, in which players armed with poles send small wooden discs scraping several yards down the deck. Passengers liable to insomnia are wise to discover before sailing if their cabin happens to be directly underneath.

Cricket at sea retains an unsullied gentlemanliness. It is played with a light plastic ball on the boat deck, the batsman's strokes severely restricted to the on- or off-side depending in which direction he is likely to give a catch to the mermaids. Sailors are remarkably keen cricket followers, despite spending most of their lives several thousand miles from the nearest blade of grass. In some of their cabins you can find enough equipment for a Test team, they oil their bats lovingly, and appear on deck in the evenings with flannels, pads, and cap to practise cuts and drives against invisible bowlers.

A ship's cricket team is welcomed by the British colony of outlandish places with the pathetic nostalgia they keep for steak-and-kidney pudding, fogs, and even, after a long enough exile, for the Commissioners of Inland Revenue. I once played a match in the middle of the Brazilian jungle at Manaos, a thousand miles up the River Amazon. The stumps we hammered into the baked mud were immovable even by the fastest bowler, there were snakes at long leg, third man was nearly eaten by a

"Listen, sir! The ship's orchestra's still playing."

jaguar, and all of us were nearly eaten by insects. But to our local compatriots, it was the Test at Lord's and Oval combined.

Horse Racing is much pleasanter at sea than ashore. Despite the absence of turf, grandstands, and the like, it is free from rain, traffic-jams, queuing for drinks, and those tedious waits between the action. A meeting is held most evenings in the smoke room, the purser rattling the dice and calling the numbers, in obedience to which half-a-dozen pretty girls in jockey caps move wooden horses down a long numbered strip of baize. Betting is on the tote system, and ten per cent is always deducted for seamen's charities. A further ten per cent is also deducted for the purser's savings, another for the head barman (who is entitled to a cut of everything below decks), another for the head steward to keep his mouth shut, and another for his mate to see he does. The steward presenting the winnings on a tray expects a tip, and it is etiquette to spend them on drinks all round.

Our great national game of *Bingo* was probably played at sea in the days of sail. There is also a daily pool on the ship's run, but never bet on "The Captain's Number"—his estimation of the ship's position is invariably so wildly out as to cast suspicions of arrival at Sydney rather than Southampton.

Water Sports are understandably popular at sea, particularly the rite of *Crossing the Line*. In this ancient and witty ceremony, all passengers facing their first change of hemisphere are led out to the swimming pool, fixed in a chair, lathered with porridge and whitewash by the Demon Barber ("Dan Druff"), dosed by the Demon Doctor with an evil mixture concocted by the ship's surgeon (which he hopes nervously is reasonably harmless), then tipped backwards and held under water by strapping young men to the point of asphyxia. The fun generally leaves a burst blood-vessel or two, assorted bruises, and occasional fracture, and is widely advertised by some shipping lines as the top diversion of the voyage.

A catalogue of ship's sports is incomplete without *Boat Drill.* This occurs precisely at four on Thursday afternoons, anticipated by the passengers as a break in the week's routine comparable with the Saturday soccer match at home. The whistle blows, the passengers don their bulky life-jackets, then make calmly and purposefully towards their boat stations. It is heartening to observe from the disciplined ranks how heavily our glorious traditions of the sea weigh upon us. Only in a British ship—with one or two regrettable exceptions like the *Titanic*—can the players feel certain of all rules being strictly observed, with women and children first and no dirty in-fighting or fouls in the scrum. Foreigners may nowadays beat us at everything else, but it is proud to reflect that at a really satisfactory shipwreck no one in the world can touch us.

Aboard a cargo boat, with less space and no girls, recreations must be largely restricted to the imagination. Sailors are keen subscribers to correspondence courses on subjects like farming, in the mind growing crops and mating bulls, or breeding mental roses and climbing mental mountains. Sadly, nobody in a cargo vessel seems to take the lead in organising games, or even regular exercise. There is absolutely nothing to do with the long, slowly chugging days across the ocean, except to find a comfortable deck chair and sleep undisturbed in the sun.

" You're certain the movies of our cruise wouldn't interest you?"

Azure seas, gentle breeze, distant lands, golden sands, heavenly views, cheap booze, are mostly between the lines in BASIL BOOTHROYD'S

Cruising Alphabet

AIR Conditioning is something cruise lines wish hadn't been invented. What with complaints either that it isn't working, or that coming in off the gale-swept sun deck into the shelter of the public rooms is like trying to find comfort in a butcher's refrigerator, they'd like to leave the customers to sweat and lump it: especially those who keep prodding the cabin installations with smuggled cutlery and setting off the sprinkler-valves by mistake. But it looks great in the advertising.

BOAT drill Don't turn up for it. No one will miss you, and if this is alarming it isn't half as bad as seeing big men ploughing through the women and children in a frenzy of self-preservation—and this only an exercise, in peril-free conditions, anyway.

CAPTAINS are notable for their Tables, which tend to accrete eminent drainage authorities, the Lady Mary Stiggins, and you if you don't watch it; also for their professional pigheadedness, which makes them sail, bang on time, in weather that would have kept Francis Drake tied up at the Hoe with extra hawsers.

DURATION should be as long as you can afford. Eight Dalmatian resorts in a four-day whiz means an unbroken roar of anchor-chains, followed by a year's marital debates on whether it was Split or Dubrovnik where you saw the eleventh century fresco with Ron Smith, Leeds, scratched across it.

"**ENTIRELY Reconverted**" is a bit of brochure talk designed to suggest trendy decor, reassuring radar equipment and top-grade seaworthiness, but it can also mean that when you open your cabin wardrobe you find it's mostly occupied by a big raw girder, giving you the unreasonable but persistent feeling that you're personally holding the whole ship together.

FLYING may be the way you have to reach the port of departure, and it's as well to check. If you're sweeping the Aegean with Epirotiki Lines, for instance—and there's nothing like Greek sailors for relaxing you in Greek waters, whereas you feel the Yugoslavs could collide with Naxos any time—it's no good hanging around Southampton expecting the *Orpheus* to sidle up. You'll find her at Piraeus: unless you forget, when directing the cab at Athens airport, that Orpheus and Piraeus both rhyme with revs.

GROOVY is what few ship's bands can be dubbed, but they make up by using enough amplifying equipment to put the generators on the blink, and even "Tea for Two" can crack a glass at twenty paces.

HORSE, Wooden Just a mention, for the souvenir-crazy, that the trinket-stalls outside Troy are selling pieces of this. Or they were last year. It could all have gone by now.

"If I remember rightly, you never asked us to your table."

"**IMMEDIATE**" is traditionally used in the daily programme of events to describe disembarkation for shore excursions, causing the deck to be packed from rail to rail, half an hour before the gangplank goes down, with a fighting mass of passengers tangled up in each other's light-meter straps and terrified of being left behind. As it's an hour after that before they're all off, bar the dead and wounded, you, who wisely aren't going, have an early choice of empty chairs. One of the finest cruise experiences is to spread out at leisure and watch the herds on the quay being sheep-dogged into their buses by the barking guides, or see the dutiful, dwindling crocodile as it disappears Hamelin fashion into the Old City of Rhodes, or toils, at the end of your binoculars, up the punishing pumice of Santorini.

"**JUST Darling**" The unvarying verdict of American ladies on all shore excursions. Also on the Captain, the squeakers issued free on Gala Night, the freighter unloading cement at the next berth, and indeed everything. Americans should get a good PRO to kill their image as fussy travellers.

KORCULA One of the chief places where no one can remember what happened there when they get home.

LIBRARY Though universally well spoken of in the cruise literature, ship's libraries aren't wholly to be relied on, partly because of eccentric opening hours, partly because there's often nothing to open but a locked metal bar across a glass-fronted shelf containing five paperbacks. In German.

"**MULTI-LINGUAL**" A courtesy adjective used of the crew, meaning that when you ask for an extra pillow they say, "Sure, OK," take away your drinking-water carafe and don't come back. This is your own fault for not speaking Croat or Albanian. And are stewards on QE 2 cruises, it's worth wondering, any more helpful at getting extra pillows for Turks? Roll on Esperanto.

NAVARONE, The Guns of This film, thanks to the sensibilities of the organisers, doesn't get many showings in ship's cinemas in the Aegean. The scene where a tempest rips up out of nowhere, reduces the ship to barrel staves and damned nearly drowns David Niven, could put thoughts into nervous heads. Bob Hope's early vehicles are more favoured, though cruise-goers of long standing avoid even those. It isn't only that it seems wrong for Hope to be up there clowning when their seats are side-slipping down a juddering trough: they just can't take "My Favourite Blonde" again.

OCTOBER Go before then because of the weather (see above). You can miss a lot of meals you've paid for in advance.

PHOTOGRAPHY is the cruiser's curse. For real enjoyment leave all cameras at home, and see Naples through your actual wide-angle human eye, instead of a little smeary view-finder. Picture-postcards do a better job anyway, and if your friends won't believe you've been there unless you're grinning in the foreground with your shirt done up on the wrong buttons, change your friends.

QUEUES These are mainly at the Purser's office, and he usually stays in his room at the back until they've gone. This doesn't apply on the last night out, when you have to keep queuing if you want to pay your bar chits. Not that you do want to, but if you don't they won't let you have your passport back. Clever.

ROMANCE, holiday Girls, remember that a tanned, sinewy officer gets upwards of six thousand melting looks per season; boys, that cute cruise hostesses are apt to be married to a tanned, sinewy officer on the sister-ship that keeps tying up alongside.

SUBMARINES A spell of service in these is ideal for adapting to average cruise cabin dimensions.

TURN-ROUND begins as soon soon as journey's end is sighted. You are then obsolete as a passenger. You've had your fun. Go. (Provided tipping has been executed).

UMBRELLAS, sun It isn't surprising, perhaps, that there's always one socket without one in. What's surprising is that it's always by the one empty chair you thought you were so smart to spot. Calomine lotion is a good substitute.

V-FORM Looking back on it all, the places you saw, the fun you had, what really lingers as sheer enjoyment is the smart way the organisers somehow managed to scrub *round* this.

WAKE, ship's obsession with movies of. See *Photography*, but if you've been fool enough to bring the cine, make a resolution to keep out of the stern. You've got enough wake footage from last year to last Robin Knox-Johnston a lifetime. Or do you think this one's different?

"We deeply regret that your cruise has been cancelled, but we are happy to offer you an immediate alternative."

XENIA Name of Greek hotels on practically all the Islands. They don't get you around like ships, but they're lovely and still. Planning for next year yet?

YARDARM No licensing laws, and not even the need to wait for the sun to be over this before breaking out with the duty-free Tom Collins? You could come back an alcoholic. Don't worry. Though ships' bars are plentiful, and look open all the time, they're only open if the man behind them is a barman, and not some other indistinguishable white-coat on mere swabbing and pistachio-sorting. No English, but a master of the mime that sends you to the bar on another deck, which mimes you back to where you came from. Cuts the liquor costs, tones the system with lots of exercise, but doesn't mean that everyone else you see hasn't managed to get a drink somewhere. A mystery of the sea.

ZURICH, Gnomes of Only to say that if Roy Jenkins is continuing the fifty quid limit to keep them happy, as it's widely bruited, they must be pretty miserable, the way we British tourists manage to line up at the ship's shop and clean it out of crocodile handbags and tape-recorders the moment we're out of the three-mile limit.

For Those in Peril on the Cruise

by GRAHAM

"**Somewhere** *on board there must be a rich divorcee.*"

"Mervyn hasn't quite got his sea legs yet."

"Is this seat taken?"

"*Oh sorry!—I was looking for the beauty salon.*"

"*Once again my early morning tea was stone cold!*"

"The sea's always been in my blood"

"Well, it's an early night for me . . . Quarter Final of the Shuffleboard Competition tomorrow."

"He's been quite good . . . what d'you think—a fiver?"

Business in Deep Waters

HAMMOND INNES on the glories of a yacht

THE footloose traveller in denims stood on the Long Pier beside me, both of us waiting for the government launch to disgorge our baggage, and I asked him where he was going. "India," he said.

"Flying?"

"No, Yacht."

"You work in India?"

He shied slightly at the word, "No-o. Boat's bound for Singapore. From there I'll pick up something going on to Perth — maybe then I'll get a job." He said it without conviction, a sop to the conventional way of life.

These are the new-style remittance men, who live tax-free and rent-free from one yacht to another on what their fathers toss their way. Girls, too, a world of footloose youngsters who drop in and drop out of any place with an anchorage, passing the time and vaguely looking for something they will probably never find.

Anyone who (for the experience, or to get to some out-of-the-way bird island) uses the services of the yacht charters, will almost certainly come across them. The world of professional sailing is now a very odd one. Not unattractive. Just not concerned with the world we live in, only in making ends meet in the way of life to which they have become addicted.

And for the youngsters who drop out in this strange fashion it's not at all a bed of roses.

Alas, they are but human. On the quays and in the bars you see them getting older. They get married, just like other people, grow up into skippers—then what was fun becomes a business. And it's hard on the girls they marry . . .

"I was cooking for ten—breakfast, lunch, dinner. That's sixty plates to wash up. They were Germans, mountains of food, then an Italian film unit, twenty-four hours to turn round, all the victualling."

Some of the skippers are also owners, men who have put what capital they had into the "£200 millionaire" dream, sailed halfway round the world to find inflation catching up with them and have turned to chartering because time has passed them by and they are not qualified to earn their living in any other way—don't want to, anyway. Touting for charters in tourist hotels and on the waterfront, they have to accept what comes, a constant invasion of their beloved boat, strangers without references,

"His compliments, Miss, and would you care to dine on the Captain's lap?"

who may be alcoholics, cardiac cases, potential suicides or just plain boors.

The most expensive charter boats are often owned by real millionaires. I lay alongside one such boat in Corfu, a huge new schooner immaculate from a Genoese yard. It was owned by an American businessman and when I asked the skipper why he bothered with charters, he said, "Oh, it's not the owner. It's the crew." He was an ocean racing man and he had just had a cracking sail, not caring overmuch that the charter party had been cabin-confined with sea-sickness. "You can't keep a team as keen as this rotting in harbour ten months of the year."

Later I saw him much further south in the little port of Gayo. He was rushing about in the yacht's speedboat, while the charter party sedately explored the village and its excellent fish restaurant. We saw him a year later in the Aegean, tramping past at 12 knots, and I envied him a little, doing pretty much what I was, but being paid for it.

And his clients—weren't they getting what they wanted, too? I went into it at the time. With accommodation for twelve on board, it worked out at slightly less per head than a luxury hotel. And luxury hotels don't take you to the remotest islands of the Aegean!

A few weeks ago, on the island of La Digue on the Indian Ocean, two of us were able to charter a well-known ocean racer for the day. We sailed to the little out-island of Grande Soeur—twin granitic peaks and in the flat land between a single planter's house built of takamaka wood. We shared our lunch with that lonely Seychellois family, using the wellhead for a table, and left laden with new-picked limes after having walked a hundred yards through the palms to the far side where the swell rolled in on to the blinding glare of a coral sand beach. Two hours later we anchored off the edge of the reef by Albatross Island, a fortress pile of rock surmounted by a few palms, went into a sheltered sandy gut in the inflatable and swam for hours as the sun went down in a kaleidoscope of piscine colour. Not in the Maldives, a thousand miles to the west, nor even on the Great Barrier Reef, have I seen such a variety of fish and water of such marvellous clarity.

All around the world now yachts provide a service, giving travellers the opportunity to explore islands and coasts and reefs not served by any other means. No matter that you feel obliged to entertain the skipper ashore, or that in places like the Mediterranean he may have his own pet restaurant where, you suspect, he gets a rake-off. No matter that drinks on board are extra and the "friends" who crew for him are often thirsty folk. It is still a world apart, the best means bar none, of getting away from it all.

How else could you possibly experience a day such as I have described in the Indian Ocean; the cost, believe it or not, was less than £9 each. And should you think, when you have fixed a charter, that perhaps you are being taken for a ride, do your sums and work out what it would set you back to have a boat of your own waiting for you with skipper and crew, ready victualled, to go to Aldabra or the Galapagos, or simply on a fortnight's cruise in Greek waters.

But don't treat a yacht as a luxury hotel. Do it for the adventure. And remember occasionally that, though you are paying, for the people who sail you it is their home. and if you think the Aegean, which is so accessible, will be full of tourists, I can only say that in three seasons in my own boat we hardly saw a soul, wandering an island world little changed since the days of Odysseus. There is no cruising ground anywhere quite so fascinating.

"I'll race you!"

SEA FEVER

by THELWELL

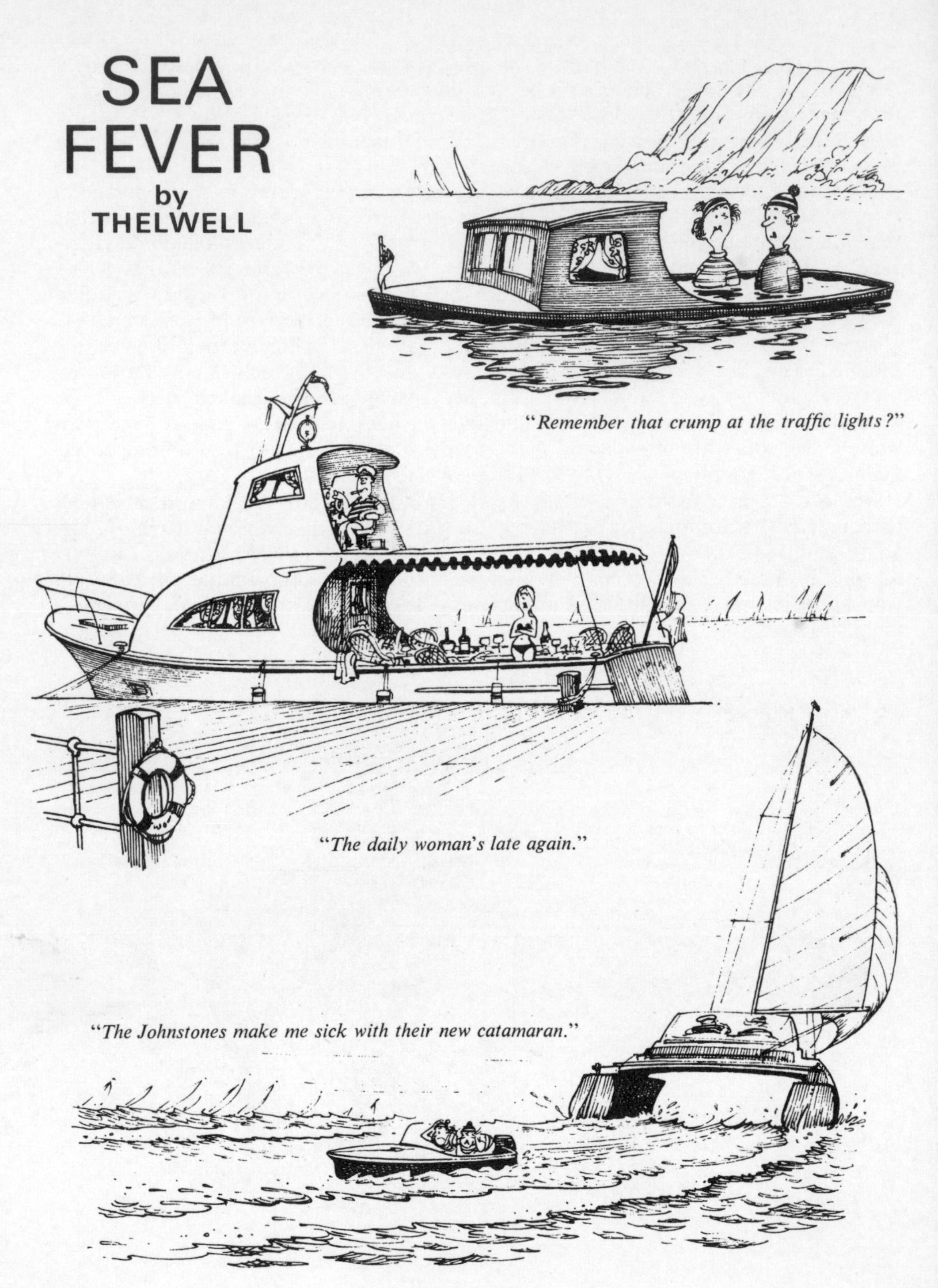

"Remember that crump at the traffic lights?"

"The daily woman's late again."

"The Johnstones make me sick with their new catamaran."

THOR HEYERDAHL

talks to DAVID TAYLOR

WHETHER or not the ancient Egyptians primed the pre-Columbian civilisations of Mexico and Peru was not, before Thor Heyerdahl, the sort of anthropological conundrum to keep people tossing in their sleep. (Nor, you might easily imagine, was the puzzle of whether foraging Peruvians had, donkey's years ago, set sail for the Polynesian islands. Yet the tale of the *Kon-Tiki* voyages has sold upwards of thirty million copies. It financed the trips on *Ra*.) Established opinion on the Egyptians was that they had stayed put where they belonged—along the banks of the Nile, idling their time as accomplished sculptors, pharaohs and mummies. Even supposing, everyone said, that they *had* made a go of fashioning boats, such boats would have been of papyrus. Papyrus is a soft, sappy, stemmy sort of reed. In the dry, it snaps; in the wet, it sinks. Over the Nile, maybe; over the Atlantic, never. The theory just didn't hold water.

The boats didn't either. It was Heyerdahl who was first to see the obvious: that a basket-weave craft drains, even in the heaviest swell. Chunks of papyrus in a tank (the hitherto accepted test of seaworthiness) will sink within days; but then, says Heyerdahl, a chunk of steel will sink still sooner and they built the QE 2 of that. He copied his design from a tomb, assembled an international crew, and a few months later cast off on perhaps the riskiest nautical gamble since the Jumblies. *Ra* 1 successfully floated but parted company with its stitching ropes two months out. *Ra* 2 was at sea for three months, more or less intact, and reached America. It was possible.

"Yes, I was frightened and no, I am not a good sailor," said Thor Heyerdahl in London as he passed through, en route for Turkey. He's still hard at work on his theories of Asia Minor transatlantic contacts and "although it is a bit early to publish anything yet, I'm getting some unbelievable material." (If it turns out that ancient Mesopotamians might well have conquered Samoa in porcelain colanders I, for one, shall not be surprised.) "I don't have any plans for a further adventure just yet, even though of course it is this which takes the public imagination. They think of me sitting on a raft, they don't think of me in a library or a museum which is where I spend most of my time. I think that perhaps I am a mixture of my two parents—my mother was an intellectual, today she would have been a scientist instead of the wife of my father; he was always seeing his son putting insects on needles and with his nose in big, heavy volumes and he was afraid that I would turn out a cissy. Always I knew that I did not want to be an academic teacher of something, I wanted to do the fieldwork."

Heyerdahl does not look the swashbuckling Captain Beefheart: he's a sensible Scandinavian, blond, sharp-featured, goes in for woolly ganseys and highly-polished brogues. He was, he admitted, a meticulous, tidy man. He's not rich, despite the successes of *Kon-Tiki*, but has poured everything back into financing his work, solo. "I am not interested in wealth. I should hate to be poor—that is not what I mean—I want only to be a free man. I'd sooner be a free hobo than tied up as a millionaire." He's found his freedom in an abandoned medieval village, high up in northern Italy,

"The typewriter! ! Lash the typewriter!"

which he bought and refurbished, Catholic church and all. "I have the Alps behind and the Mediterranean in front. I begin work at 7.30 and go on uninterrupted until 6. Then perhaps I will strip off and go out into the forest with an axe or on a mule, working so hard until I sweat. Nature to me is my god. If you ask me if I am religious I would say yes. A lot of other people would say I was definitely not. It means only that I don't see my god in a long, white gown with sandals and a beard."

An accomplished linguist (he can get along in Italian, French, German, English, Spanish and Polynesian as well as his native Norwegian), Heyerdahl is absorbed by man. "I don't distinguish clearly between men of different races, nor between man today and 5,000 years ago. I do respect Darwin, of course, but I think evolution can be exaggerated as a development in man. In the Galapagos, on Easter Island, talking to Moslems, talking to you: the patterns all to me are similar. Even the astronauts—before I met them I thought they must be supermen. Now I think that, with training, I wouldn't be afraid to attempt what they did. But I wouldn't be tempted. Our own planet is the one with tremendous interest, I would far sooner, for instance, undertake a mission to the bottom of the oceans. If you want to know what really upsets me, it is the state of the oceans, the pollution that *every day* we observed from *Ra.* We have got to do something about that. And do it quickly. That, apart from aeroplanes, is what frightens me."

Lock, Pint and Barrel

by BILL TIDY

Sam Hinchcliffe's Canal Holiday

"Call me a romantic fool, luv, but I've decided to drink me way single-handed round British Waterways' pubs."

"He filled the log in before he left!"

"*Of course this is how it's done. I checked with that man over there.*"

"*Don't look so surprised, sweetie. We've been marked on the charts since 1937!*"

"Easy, Sarge, there's not a lot we can do about it."

"Do you know what, luv . . . I think I'm doomed to sail these canals for ever."

ENGLAND EXPECTS . . .

The Royal Navy has run desperately short of spare parts, replacements and new equipment. To greet the birth of a new naval tradition, MILES KINGTON updates some old sea yarns

DON Jose Ignacio Jaime Ferdinando Manuel Rodrigo Pascual de Sanchez y de la Concepcion, as his friends called him for short, stood on the poop deck of the stately Spanish galleon, *La Reina de España*, and gazed uncomprehendingly at the blue sea. Five more days before the galleon reached Spain with its burden of gold, diamonds, silver, tobacco, chocolate and the curious substance that the natives called chewing gum. At least, five days was what the mate told him, but it was beyond Don Jose how such a firm figure could be reached when all there was in sight was blue sea. Don Jose was captain of *La Reina de España*, but he was no sailor; this was a prestige position given to him as a nobleman to avoid the dangers of having a low-born sailor in charge, and he hated it. He found no pleasure in ordering lashings to be given to mutinous sailors. He would much rather have been at home, ordering lashings for recalcitrant peasants.

Don Jose stuffed another wad of chewing gum into his pipe and lit it, though personally he found little pleasure in this strange custom. He stared at the sea again. Nothing but water. Not a thing, unless you counted that tiny dot on the horizon . . .

That tiny dot on the horizon? Don Jose ordered a telescope to be brought. He asked an officer to look through it. He ordered the officer to report what he saw.

"It is a ship, Señor," said the officer, "but too far off to identify. Let us pray to

St. Joseph that it is not an English ship. These British sea dogs are the fiercest and cruellest on the ocean."

St. Joseph, it seemed, had better things to do, because half an hour later it became clear to all that the mystery ship was flying a British flag, tattered and drab. It was sailing very slowly, almost drifting.

"Should we try to escape?" said Don Jose, who liked to pretend an interest in navigation.

"It is useless, Senor," said the officer. "These pirates sail like the wind. Better surrender and save life."

Gradually the British ship came alongside. A solitary grappling iron was flung towards *La Reina*. It missed and fell in the water.

"Damn!" came a loud clear English voice. "'Fraid that's our last one, chaps. You'll have to swim. Sorry, and all that."

The English crew swarmed down the side, swam across the gap and swarmed up the corresponding side. Five minutes later, it was all over.

"Will you accept my sword in defeat?" said Don Jose to the English captain.

"I certainly will," said Sir Francis Drake. "Five months I've been waiting for my new one to come through and been reduced to fighting with an old walking stick meanwhile. Feel damned stupid, not hitting the enemy too hard in case it breaks. Well, can't stand here chatting all day. Must loot the ship, I'm afraid. Thanks for the sword. Can't spare the dagger, can you?"

"It is a present from my wife," said Don Jose stiffly.

"Ah, well keep it then," said Sir Francis. "I had a dagger too once. Present from Queen Elizabeth. She asked for it back after six months—weren't enough to go round and it was Sir Walter's turn to wear it. Right lads—pillage and sack! If we've still got a sack," he added.

Half an hour later, the English ship was sailing away, still very slowly. Too late,

"It's now or never if we're going to have a mutiny."

the Spaniards realised this was because they had no sails, only large masts.

"Captain!" shouted the officer. "I have been down to the treasure hold. The English have left all the gold and silver—nothing has been touched."

"Then what in Mary's name have they taken?" wondered Don Jose, as the British ship drifted away, laden down with precious Spanish marline-spikes, biscuits, rope, screws, thread, shoes and maps, and flying a brand-new Spanish flag.

II

After thirty-two years of being marooned on this island, I Robinson Crusoe, today saw another sail. Words cannot express the joy with which I witnessed fellow white men, Englishmen, come ashore on the beach which had always before been trod by cannibals and savages.

At first they drew back in alarm at the strange figure I cut, but reassured by my English voice, though rusty at first, they clapped me on the shoulder.

"I'll be jiggered!" cried one. "An Englishman! What the devil are you doing in the Dutch East Indies?"

"The Dutch Indies? But they are four thousand miles from here!" I cried.

"The devil they are," said another. "That's what comes of navigating without a map."

"What is this strange idea, to sail without a map?" I inquired.

"Oh Lord! Here he goes again."

"*Well you had no* **right** *to give the port side a day off!*"

"Don't ask me, mate, ask the Admiralty. They can't get the maps, they tell us. Similarly sextants, compasses and logbooks. I tell you, it's getting on my nerves, memorising the log instead of writing it down. Not to mention doing without ropes. When I joined the Navy, I didn't expect to have to climb aloft by cutting steps in the mast. Bleedin' lucky to get a mast at all, they told us. They did think of converting the ship to a bleedin' rowin' galley. But they couldn't get the bleedin' oars, of course."

"Never mind," I cried. "Give me but five minutes to pack and I will come aboard to meet the captain and the crew."

The four of them eyed each other.

"There's just us," said one. "We was expecting more crew but they couldn't find anyone."

"Is there no press gang still?" I asked.

"Press gang?" They laughed. "Can't get a press gang for love nor money. Never mind, mate. Get your stuff and come with us."

It was then that I noticed with a sinking heart that the ship in the bay was not so near as it had been.

"Look," I cried.

"For crying out loud," exclaimed one. "Didn't you anchor the damn thing, Johnson?"

"Very funny," said Johnson. "And who ordered the anchor to be melted down for cannon balls last week?"

"Ah," said the leader. "Well, we all make mistakes. Never mind, we can make

"Where's this place mate?"

ourselves comfy here while we're waiting for a replacement ship."

They stood watching the vessel float away into the open sea, while I began to resign myself to the thought of another thirty years on this isle.

III

"Mr. Christian!" said Captain Bligh. "What you are saying amounts to treason and mutiny. I give you one more chance to reconsider."

"About all you have given us," said Christian. "Ever since we set sail, if you can call ship's blankets sewn together sail, you have kept us short of everything a crew should have. Low rations, no equipment, rotten meat, sub-standard clothing, no grog . . . ."

"I am no magician," said Bligh. "They are all on order."

"You have given the crew unmerciful lashings," said Christian.

"But only with a cat o' three tails," said Bligh hopefully.

"You pushed a man overboard."

"I made him walk the plank, which was unfortunately missing."

"We therefore have decided to cast you adrift in the ship's boat, together with such sailors as wish to go with you. I have no more to say."

Silently, the mutineers swung the gig out and let it fall into the ocean where, rotted by years of woodworm and lack of maintenance, it fell to bits and sank.

"Look at that," said Christian bitterly. "You can't even give us a decent boat to set you adrift in."

"Then you'll let me stay?" said Bligh eagerly.

"Well . . ." said Christian doubtfully. "You won't put all this down in the log?"

"With the last pencil eaten by mice three days ago?" said Bligh.

"Then . . . no Mutiny on the Bounty?"

"Cross my heart," said Bligh.

IV

The two ships, one French, one English, drew so close together that the captains could address each other.

"You are not French?" said the French captain. "I was misled by the name of your ship. But you are flying a flag of greeting."

"It was meant to be a distress flag," said the English captain. "But we haven't got one. The thing is, we've broken down. Can't move. We need help."

"Broken down?" said the Frenchman, surprised. "You have sails, though."

"Fat lot of good that is without a steering wheel. It broke free this morning and rolled overboard. It was only held on by one nut. And everything else on this damned ship is going wrong. Can you take us on board to the nearest port?"

"Of course," said the French captain affably. "Come with us and you will soon be back in England."

They never were, though. Everyone, from captain to cabin boy, was so impressed with the efficiency and equipment of the French navy that before sighting land they had all decided to join up and leave the English fleet. They abandoned their ship and never went back, but nobody minded; in the words of the cabin boy: "I won't be sorry if I never see the *Mary Celeste* again."

"Hold it: Harry's got cramp!"

and a star to steer her by . . .

Life afloat as seen by earlier cartoonists

HOW VERY THOUGHTFUL

Old Lady. "Are you not afraid of getting drown'd when you have the boat so full?"

Boatman. "Oh, dear, no, mum. I always wears a life-belt, so I'm safe enough."

TOO SOLID.

Skipper. "DID YE GOT THE PROVEESIONS ANGUS?"
Angus. "AY, AY! A HALF LOAF, AN' FOUER BOTTLES O' WHISKEY."
Skipper. "AN' WHAT IN THE WOARLD WILL YE BE DOIN' WI' AAL THAT BREAD?"

A PLEDGED M.P.

M.P.'s Bride. "OH! WILLIAM, DEAR—IF YOU ARE—A LIBERAL—DO BRING IN A BILL—NEXT SESSION—FOR THAT UNDERGROUND TUNNEL!!"

Mr. Dibbles (*at Balham*). "AH, THE OLD CHANNEL TUNNEL SCHEME KNOCKED ON THE HEAD AT LAST! GOOD JOB TOO! MAD-HEADED PROJECT—BEASTLY UN-PATRIOTIC TOO!"

Mr. Dibbles (*en route for Paris. Sea choppy*). "CHANNEL TUNNEL NOT A BAD IDEA. ENTIRE JOURNEY TO PARIS BY TRAIN. GRAND SCHEME! ENGLISH PEOPLE BACKWARD IN THESE KIND OF THINGS. STEWARD!" [*Goes below.*

"DOWN IN THE DEEP."

FUN AT HENLEY REGATTA. BERTIE ATTEMPTS TO EXTRICATE HIS PUNT FROM THE CROWD.

BIS DAT QUI CITO DAT.

Lock-keeper (handing ticket). "THREEPENCE, PLEASE."
Little Jenkins. "NOT ME: I'VE JUST PAID THAT FELLOW BACK THERE."
Lock-keeper (drily). "'IM? OH, THAT 'S THE CHAP *WHO COLLECTS FOR THE BAND!*"

HOPE DEFERRED.

Jones (*who is not feeling very well*). "How long did you say it would take us to get back?"
Boatman. "'Bout 'n 'our an' a 'arf agin this Tide."

Mothers Pet. "Oh, there's ma on the beach, looking at us, Alfred ; let's make the boat lean over tremendously on one side ! "

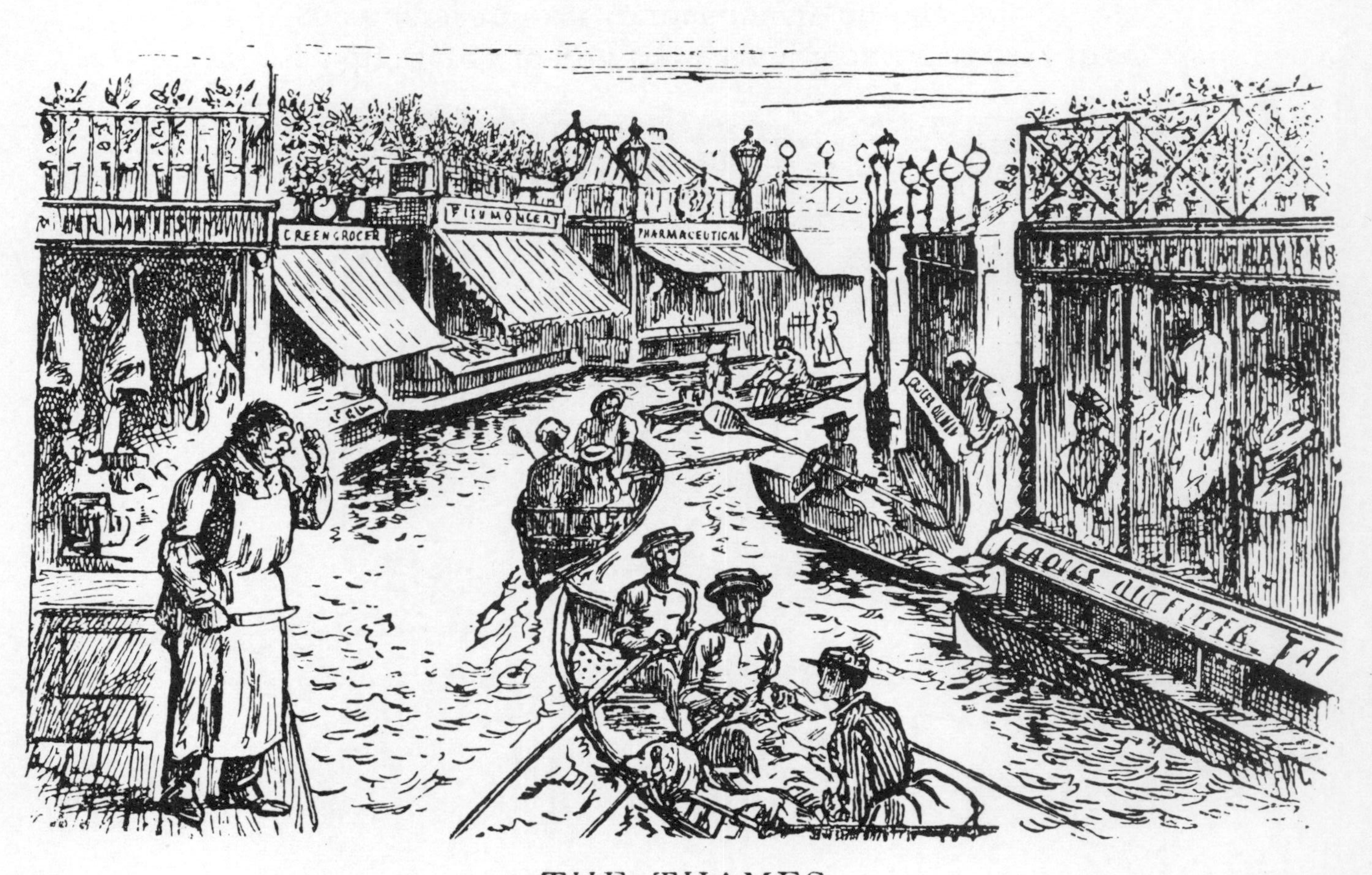

THE THAMES
(Development of the house-boat system)

TRIALS OF A NOVICE.

Extract from Diary.—"WEDNESDAY. WENT FOR A SPIN OR TRIP, OR WHATEVER IT 'S CALLED, ON BOWLINES' NEW RACING YACHT. FELT VERY NERVOUS WHEN WE TURNED THE CORNERS; NEARLY FELL OVERBOARD WHILE I WAS TRYING TO BALANCE THE THING; THOUGHT WE SHOULD HAVE BEEN DROWNED. B. SAID IT WAS A WONDER WE WEREN'T—THANKS TO *ME!* HAD A FEW WORDS WITH B. *Mem.*—NEVER AGAIN!"

[*N.B.*—*B. says the same.*

"EXEMPLI GRATIA"

Ancient Mariner (*to credulous yachtsman*). "A'miral Lord Nelson! Bless yer, I knowed him; served under him. Many's the time I've as'ed him for a bit o' 'bacco, as I might be a astin' o' you; and says he, 'Well, I ain't got no 'bacco,' jest as you might say to me; 'but here's a shillin' for yer,' says he"!!

Malicious Swell in the stern sheets (*to little party on the weather quarter*). Splendid breeze, isn't it, Gus?"

Gus (*who, you see, has let his cigar go out*). "Ye-es; but I say, what's o'clock? Isn't it time to turn back?—What d'ye think?"

EASTER RECREATIONS.

Enthusiastic Skipper (to friend). "AH, MY BOY! THIS IS WHAT YOU WANTED. IN A SHORT TIME YOU 'LL FEEL YOURSELF A DIFFERENT MAN!"

The Margate excursion boat arrives at 2.30 p.m., after a rather boisterous passage.

Ticket Collector (*without any feeling*). "Ticket, sir! Thankye, sir! Boat returns at 3!"

OVERHEARD ON AN ATLANTIC LINER.

She (*on her first Trip to Europe*). "I GUESS YOU LIKE LONDON?"
He. "WHY, YES. I GUESS I KNOW MOST PEOPLE IN LONDON. I WAS OVER THERE LAST FALL!"

GOOD RESOLUTIONS.

Blenkinsop (on a Friend's Yacht) soliloquises. "I know one thing, if ever I'm rich enough to keep a Yacht, I shall spend the Money in Horses."

Hello Weekend Sailor

JONATHAN SALE signs up with the amateur yachtsmen

AS soon as the first ever dugout was sent splashing into the first pond, it must have been hauled out and pressed into service as the bar of the yacht club that was founded on the spot. Indeed, it may have happened the other way round. Since then, the signing of banker's orders payable to the club has been as essential as casting off for pleasure sailors worthy of the name.

Today's sailing societies range from the Royal Yachting Association—the TUC of amateur boating, although neither organisation will thank me for the comparison —to the specialised groups such as the Enterprise Association, which exists not for go-getting young businessmen to gather together, but for the mutual interests of owners of Enterprise class dinghies.

Dinghies proper are comfortable only for an afternoon's racing, if that. Those owning craft large enough for living on join the Cruising Association, which goes back to a meeting in a certain Bay Tree Tavern in 1908. It has come a long way since then, and now "The CA Council keeps a weather eye open for encroachments of the freedom of the seas" and its burgee (the 24-inch nylon version costs £1.20, 5p extra for Terylene/wool, plus postage) "has rounded Cape Horn".

Less strenuous activities include the consulting of its 10,000 books, which may be borrowed so long as you return them within a fortnight and don't "take them on board ship"—well, they could so easily get wet—and socials: "Members will be invited aboard Host Boat KURI MOANA, flying the CA ensign at the mizzen masthead, from 1730 onwards for drinks." They award prizes for logs of trips, and one published in a recent *Bulletin* shows that Women's Lib has taken to the water: "*The Skipper*—my Mother, Mrs. Fiona Bond. *Navigation Officer*—my father, Major Alan Bond." Other parts were played by "*First Mate*—myself, Rosalind (16 years)" and "*Midshipman*—Jonathan (9) years."

The least clubable of sailing clubs specialise in traditional gaff-rigged boats with their four-sided sails, as opposed to the modern triangular—Bermudan—rig. Many of the boats its members now sail were launched at the turn of the century, but it wasn't until 1963 that people got together to place things on a formal fitting thus: "1. NAME. The name of the Association shall be THE OLD GAFFERS ASSOCIATION. 2. OBJECTS. The objects of the Association shall be to encourage interest in traditional gaff rig. 3. BURGEE. The Association Burgee shall be white with a blue pitchfork." From time to time they honour a member with the title of "Elder Gaffer" which frees him from payment of subs.

"Piratical individualists" is how the East Coast Secretary described members to me. "They don't even want to get together on a starting line."

Those that manage to lower the Jolly Roger for long enough to stay in the race are eligible for prizes, the awarding of which shows the Old Gaffers in the most endearing of lights. Take the forthcoming Solent race in September.

An entrant may miss out on the first two prizes. Okay, he's third, he gets

*"I wanted you on **this** side."*

the "Gaffer's Eye" prize. (This sounds like the first draft of a translation of the Bible: It is easier for a dromedary to pass through the eye of a gaffer than . . .) But if he is in the *last* boat to cross the *starting* line, he gets a prize, as does the last boat to complete the course, in this case the "Laggard's Ladle". But if, by the accident of going too fast, he avoids this, he may be eligible for the "Pitchfork"—provided that his boat hails from the most far distant port.

Not Elder Gaffer but "Admiral" is the title of the top man at the Enterprise Association, which is one of the countless fleets confined to one sort of dinghy. Other services offered include the chance of being elected to Vice or Rear Commodore, and a selection of leaflets on cutting transom draining holes and suchlike. The Association also offers insurance cover for up to £100,000, which provides a fair scope for the aquatic vandal.

There are other land-based hazards besides insurance that take to the water, and "marine mortgages" are available for anyone who finds the thrills and spills of the repayments on his house not exciting enough. These come courtesy of the Royal Yachting Association, which also offers pamphlets on racing rules, amendments to pamphlets on racing rules, and full details on "Weather Vocabulary in Seven Languages", the last of which might seem unnecessary until you ask yourself, "Do *I* speak Weather like a native?" and realise that there is scope for a language course with records and broadcasts.

It would be a rash helmsman who upped anchor without his "pad of 25 protest forms", kept handy for filling in and shoving in a bottle if the craft is sliced in two by a hit-and-run tanker. And before you go down for the last time, don't forget to rescue your RYA cuff links in gold and silver, lapel badge with pin or bar, car badge, blazer badge, key ring, set of twelve reefer buttons and powder compact complete with RYA motif.

The powder compact reminds us, at least, those of us who watched the recent Smack and Sailing Barge Match on the Thames, of one of the umpires. According

"How am I doing?"

"Have you finished with the Sunday papers?"

to the organisers, the Society for Spritsail Barge Research and the Kentish Sail Association: "The world of London's tideway is not just confined to men. Umpiring the Match for punts (50 ton oared lighters) . . . 'Mother Thames' herself—octogenarian Mrs. Dorothea 'Dolly' Woodard-Fisher O.B.E." After the prizegiving under the bowsprit of the Cutty Sark, the crews were feasted on "a traditional meal of 'salt horse' as was served to the clipper ship men themselves" and besides which the Horn itself must have held few fears.

Another focus for nautical scholars is the Amateur Yacht Research Society. This engages in high-powered discussions on craft design, and its publications discuss aspects such as the place of the rudder in twentieth century yachts (yes, the stern, but there's more to it than that). Also, do whales bump into lone yachtsmen by mistake, or with malice aforethought? Finally, "George Patterson, the inventive cat designer" (catamaran, of course) "has come up with a sailing bike." As seen in

"Simpson . . . Eric Simpson, you remember, we were at training school together."

their picture of man on port tack with Bermudan sail on mast fixed above the front, no, bow, wheel.

If that seems dismissive, let me point out that sailing on dry land has an honourable history: remains of a sand yacht were discovered among the possessions of a Pharoah of the XII Dynasty, and the first one in Europe was the work of a Dutchman in 1595, whose design enabled ten men to be propelled by the power of two galleon sails. At the start of the twentieth century, sand yachts could be hired by the hour, and Bleriot was just one of the customers who used to enjoy a spin. In England the sport, stopped by the First and then the Second World War, took off again with one club on an aerodrome in Huntingdonshire and another on a beach near Blackpool. The two got together to form the British Federation of Sand and Land Yacht Clubs, and the rest is history.

"On average it takes six hours of sailing to qualify for a pilot's licence," writes Tony Ferrand in the Federation's introductory leaflet. Although a new boat (craft? vehicle?) may cost nearly £600, there is no extra expenditure on petrol or harbour dues. "The beach is your oyster," he concludes, "and the wind is free."

Finally, a word of caution. Amateur boating is fun, but contains its share of human suffering. All that is left of the Yacht and Motor Boat Association is a bleak mention in a list of assorted organisations, just above the Yeovil Agricultural Society: "Please delete." Alas, went down with all members.

Weekend with the Boss

Ted Heath may have come up with something new in labour relations when he asked the Institute of Directors "How often do you take your Trade Union Leaders out on your boat?" But MAHOOD foresees some snags in this approach

"At least old George is determined not to be compromised."

"Oh dear, I was hoping for the pleasure of Brother Ackroyd's company."

"Your 'Morning Star', sir."

"They like to keep themselves to themselves."

"Don't sign anything yet—I think we're getting a better offer from Sir Reginald of Amalgamated."

"Wait till the Industrial Relations Board hears about **this,** *Ackroyd!"*

"For God's sake, Hoskins, can't you even decide whether to have red or white wine without consulting Clive Jenkins?"

"Dammit, I came here to get away from the office."

The Compleat Melly

FOR most of the year, working—drinking—telephoning—worrying—neurotically tidying objects—making and breaking appointments and resolutions—eating too much—spending too much—saying "yes" when I should say "no" and "no" when I should say "yes"—feeling impotently angry or dangerously euphoric — several times a day for most of the year I resort, to keep sane, to my own personal mantra, the word "fishing".

"Fishing", I think, and then the crowded party, the blank sheet of paper, the second helping of *crême brulée* recede.

I see myself, clumsy in thigh waders, crossing a field; watching for the first sight and sound of the water, the rosy evening light fading, the liquid shadows under the trees on the far bank darkening; the first bat, expected but never at exactly *that* moment skittering out of the sky, to signal that it's time to start fishing seriously; the balance between detached calm and childishly excited anticipation as the fly drops more or less where I wanted it to and floats, without dragging, down the pool; the incredible moment when the first frantic tug and splash of a sea trout is followed by the scream of a reel as the fish makes its first run and the rod bends and quivers; the anxiety and excitement which lasts right up until it turns on its side and is in the net; the triumphant ride home through the dark on my maxi-putsch moped.

Writing about fishing is probably a dead loss. People who fish know what I get out of it already. Those that don't are divided between the "it's so cruel" and the "it's so boring" schools of thought. I've no answer to the former except the arguments that make me snort with scorn when I hear them used in defence of hunting. Given that the tackle has a fairly low breaking-point, the fish has a chance to get away. But it doesn't *know* that and clearly by the way it fights it's not enjoying being caught at all. Of course it's quickly killed (with a blunt instrument called "a priest", a fact which always feeds my anti-clericism), and is eaten, but catching it is what's so marvellous and don't believe anyone who says the real point is being in the presence of nature—it usually just means they've had a poor week.

Therefore it's better just to own up. I like fishing because I like it. The drawn-out anticipation and the excitement add up to something which I find so satisfactory that it anaesthetises any qualms I may have about the creature's suffering, and if that makes me the Marquis de Sade in waders, it's just too bad.

As to the tedium, well there isn't any, and despite what I've just written I do find what they intended to call "communion with nature", though secondary, a part of it. To move slowly down a stretch of river means seeing, in pre-Raphaelite detail, more than all but the most committed naturalist: the trees or wild flowers, dragonflies, water rats, weasels and stoats and, best of all, that mad tropical flash of a kingfisher.

Then, too, the equipment is so delicate and subtle. To put up a rod, especially a split-cane rod, to choose flies from a box, many of them tied by my father, to make up a cast, and all this slowly, contemplatively, while keeping half an eye on the water for the swirl and spreading rings of a big fish beginning to feed, and then to get up, with a damp bum from the bank, and creep towards the river's edge and begin to cast

There is too, if one knows a river well, a choice of where to go. In Wales, on the

"Some hooligan's altered the clock again."

Teivi where I fish most often, I've a choice of about six favourite stretches. One, the nearest, has two good pools but is quite ugly. There's a nasty pumping station and a lot of villas, but it is a good place for the sea trout or sewin as the Welsh call them.

A mile further up on the opposite bank is a place I call the "false Empson stretch". It gained this strange name because it was near some water owned by the poet William Empson when he was living there and my wife, in the days before I'd passed my moped test, frequently got the two confused when she came to pick me up in the car.

"The false Empson stretch" can be good but tends to be unnerving. Once I looked up from the water to see a large bull snorting down on the bank above me. It turned out to be perfectly amiable but I didn't enjoy walking back to the gate.

More sinister, in fact downright terrifying, was when the tip of my rod knocked a bat into the river and it swam, apparently malevolently, towards me, and even flapped after me across the stones when I finally and almost hysterically retreated out of the water. Later a naturalist told me that, as a warm solid object, it probably fixed me with its radar as the best thing to aim at. I ran though. No, although I've often done well there, "the false Empson stretch" is a bit jinxy.

The best stretch of all is a half mile of water far from the road—you cross a narrow tributary, walk along a lane, cross three fields and it's there. A heron flaps clumsily up as I approach, It's wild, and the opposite bank is steep with gorse and tall trees. There's a dusk pool, and a long bit of rough water to fish until it gets dark. It's difficult wading and impossible when the water's high. I'm entirely alone, never bored, far from the madding crowd, the madding telephone, the madding "Dear George Melly; I realise you're very busy, but . . ." It's all there waiting.

"That was a near thing, Mavis."

MY FINEST HOUR

RICHARD GORDON tells a saga of the sea

FRUSTRATED ambitions are essential nourishment for our self-esteem. I know that I should have made a terrible Naval officer. I am totally undisciplined and bad at trigonometry. But I was desperate for a Naval career, since being taken to a matinee of *The Middle Watch* at the Shaftesbury Theatre in 1929. In my childhood dreams I stood on the bridge, telescope under arm, quietly mastering such perils as shipwreck, mutiny, yellow jack, fire down below, and icebergs, quelling the panic on deck with a curt, "Women and children first."

As disabilities (largely psychosomatic) barred me from the Royal Navy, once I qualified I settled for the second-best and joined the Merchant one. There was no such undignified formality as a physical examination before becoming a doctor in a merchant ship, you just hung round the lines' offices like any other unemployed sailor. As no British vessel over ninety-nine souls aboard is allowed to sail without a medical officer, and as at that time just after the war ships' doctors had suddenly become as scarce as Liberal MPs, the first office I tried pretty well Shanghaied me on the spot.

My ship was apparently rather older than myself, and had already finished one useful life ferrying soldiers and sahibs to India. She was now about to leave for Australia with some five hundred passengers, middle-class refugees from Mr. Attlee's brave new world. I was too jubilant to worry about the vessel's amenities, or even seaworthiness, as they instructed me to join her at Victoria Docks in a week's time. Then they sent me to the shipping registry in the Minories, which I found to combine the atmosphere of a busy post office and a police station on a Saturday night, where someone looked up the *Register* to see if I was a proper doctor, fingerprinted me, and took my photograph with a number in a frame under my chin. This turned out nearer my conception of Jack the Ripper than Jack Tar, but I was compensated with an identity card officially describing me as a "seafarer." After my childhood fantasies, it was comparable with actually driving the Flying Scotsman or shooting the winning goal at Wembley.

Doctors employed by Leadenhall Street rather than the Admiralty are obliged to find their own gear, but unhappily like all newly-qualified ones, my financial lifeblood was sadly anaemic. The long-desired blue uniform was bought for two pounds in a pub, from a friend just demobilised as a surgeon-lieutenant. I thought the scuffed gold braid and trail of pink-gin stains down the front gave it a satisfyingly deep-water look. The high-necked tropical "whites" came second-hand from a theatrical costumers, and had doubtless appeared in several amateur productions of *The Middle Watch*, I found a chauffeur's cap in Soho, added the tie which I kept for funerals, put it all on, and looked in the mirror. To my own eyes, I was as much a sailor as Nelson on top of his column.

The exciting morning arrived for me to go aboard. I said an early farewell to my landlady in Pimlico, picked up my suitcase (which I referred to as my "ditty-box"),

"If there's one thing I insist on—it's a happy ship."

and took the Tube to Canning Town. Only then did misgivings assail me. The Royal Navy provides its medical officers with elaborate instruction to adapt themselves to the physical and social hazards of their new environment. The rougher Merchant Service runs on the principle that once aboard the lugger everything will somehow work itself out. I realised that I didn't know the difference between starboard and leeward, I couldn't tell a chronometer from a dog-watch, and I was equally ignorant of the precise functions of the capstan and the captain. But timidity faded as I stumbled across the dockside railway lines and caught sight of the thin, upright funnels of my ship, poking above the warehouses. I already felt beckoning those empty blue horizons which had enticed Sir Francis Drake and Captain Cook. With the tide (that seemed the phrase) I should be heading for the open sea and the Antipodes.

I hurried up a steep, insecure-looking gangway. At the top sat an old man, smoking a pipe, I announced that I was the new ship's doctor. He hauled up his trouser-leg and invited my opinion on his knee. I suggested aspirin, and demanded to see the officer of the watch. He said I could try the cabins under the bridge, mate, but he reckoned everyone was having breakfast.

I found a young man in his pyjamas, shaving in a glass surrounded by photographs of bulbous nudes. To be on the safe side, I saluted smartly. He looked surprised,

". . . and stop calling me 'Mr. Christian!'"

and offered me a pink gin, which I later discovered to be the more normal form of salutation aboard. He explained that he was the Third Officer, and to get rid of me suggested that I toured the ship.

As I wandered aft, I first noticed that the vessel was largely in pieces. The decks were luttered with pipes, girders, sliced ventilators, riveted plates, and quite substantial sections of machinery. Instead of sailors, the ship was alive with arc-welders and carpenters. Instead of bos'n's' pipes, there came the periodic scream of tortured metal. I looked over the side. No sea. No oil-streaked threshold of the oceans. Just concrete, a disconcertingly long way below. We were in dry-dock, as incapable of sailing to Australia as the Houses of Parliament.

We stayed there for six weeks. They were the finest of my life. I was being paid at generous ocean-going rates. I drew my ration of duty-free tobacco and gin. I ate magnifiicent meals—seafarers always do themselves well, perhaps in compensation for eighteenth-century privations. In the evenings, I caught the Tube back to my Pimlico haunts. Wearing my uniform, exclusively drinking pink gin, I expanded heartily in my favourite pubs on the joys and hardships of a sailor's life. I began to imagine that from nine to five every day I was really outward bound for Sydney, though there seemed no possibility of even the most able marine engineer ever putting my ship together again.

But one morning the bits were fitted together somehow, smoke came from the funnels, stewards roamed in clean white jackets, winches rattled, flags flew, the Captain paced the bridge, and my spirits fell. I loved being a sailor. But I didn't want to go to sea at all. It would be noisy and draughty, and I should certainly be seasick. Even in dry-dock I had felt definitely queasy. And boat drill would be held as we reached the storm-tossed waters of the Channel. It is always punctual aboard British vessels, because we are as a nation rather good at shipwrecks, lovingly remembering some splendid ones in our history, when everyone drowned with impeccable manners and undampened good humour. As I could hardly "jump ship" before we had even left port, I should be standing the next morning by my lifeboat, in full view of the passengers, disgracing myself.

I had a cruel choice. I could try and see out boat-drill, by thinking fixedly of some terrestial feature like the Albert Hall. Or I could be a coward, and take some sea-sickness pills. I hesitated until the alarm bells sounded, then fell. Unfortunately, like most in the ship's hospital, the label on the bottle had long ago become unreadable, so I swallowed a handful and hoped for the best.

I stood on deck, cap at a rakish angle, facing the greenish passengers in their life-jackets. I was beautifully eupeptic. The image of myself as a seafarer, which could so easily that morning have been shattered beyond repair, at last came into full focus with my childish vision. If I had cheated, that mattered less and less as the passengers steadily slumped and wilted. I was a sailor, the deck might heave, but I didn't.

But in my haste I had forgotten my basic pharmacology, that an overdose of the drug hyoscine in seasick pills could induce disturbances of vision, staggering, dis-organised behaviour, incoherent speech, and outbursts of wild laughter. For the rest of the voyage the passengers pointedly avoided me professionally or socially, and the Captain kept trying to smell my breath. A humiliating sequel to a fine moment, I thought bitterly at the time, But the wound healed. It hardly took more than a couple of voyages before I discovered that a ship's doctor drunk at nine in the morning was a matter far less worthy of knowing comment than one being seasick down his brass buttons.

"It's awfully hard to get decent help nowadays."

For Those in Peril on The Broads

THELWELL takes a look at Norfolk's floating chaplain

"She's brand new. We'd like you to christen her."

"They'll allow me to bury you at sea but not in these waters, I'm afraid."

"I didn't see you in church today, Mr. Rigby."

BUBBLE

A ghost story by HAMMOND INNES

SHE lay in Kinlochbervie in the north-west of Scotland, so cheap I should have known there was something wrong. I had come by way of Lairg, under the heights of Arkle, and four miles up the road that skirts the north shores of Loch Laxford I turned a corner and there she was—a ketch painted black and lying to her own reflection in the evening sun.

Dreams, dreams . . . dreams are fine, as an escape, as a means of counteracting the pressures of life in a big office. But when there is no barrier between dream and reality, what then? Draw back, create another dream? But one is enough for any man and this had been mine; that one day I would find the boat of my dream and sail her to the South Seas.

Maybe it was the setting, the loneliness of the loch, the aid of Nordic wildness with the great humped hills of Sutherland as backcloth and the mass of Arkle cloud-capped in splendour. Here the Vikings had settled. From here men only just dead sailed open boats south for the herring. Even her name seemed right—*Samoa.*

I bought her, without a survey, without stopping to think. And then my troubles started.

She was dry when I bought her. Nobody told me the agents had paid a man to pump her out each day. If my wife had been alive I would never have been such a fool. But it was an executor's sale. The agents told me that. Also that she had been taken in tow off Handa Island by a Fraserburgh trawler and was the subject of a salvage claim. With her port of registry Kingston, Jamaica, it explained the low asking price. What they didn't tell me was that the trawler had found her abandoned, drifting waterlogged without a soul on board. Nor did they tell me that her copper sheathing was so worn that half her underwater planking was rotten with toredo.

"A wee bit of a mystery," was the verdict of the crofter who helped me clean her up and pump the water out of her. Nobody seemed to know who had sailed her across the Atlantic, how many had been on board, or what had happened to them.

The first night I spent on board—I shall always remember that; the excitement, the thrill of ownership, of command, of being on board a beautiful ship that was also now my home. The woodwork gleamed in the lamplight (yes, she had oil lamps as well as electric light), and lying in the quarter berth I could look up through the open hatch to the dark shape of the hills black against the stars. I was happy in spite of everything, happier than I had been for a long time, and when I finally went to sleep it was with a picture of coral islands in my mind—white sands and palm strees and proas scudding across the pale green shallows of warm lagoons.

I woke shivering, but not with cold. It was a warm night and the cold was inside me. I was cold to my guts and very frightened. It wasn't the strangeness of my new habitation, for I knew where I was the instant I opened my eyes. And it wasn't fear of the long voyage ahead. It was something else, something I didn't understand.

I shifted to one of the saloon berths, and as I slept soundly the rest of the night I

put it down to nerves. It was a nervous breakdown that had led to my early retirement, enabling me to exchange my small suburban house for the thing I had always dreamed of. But I avoided the quarter berth after that, and though I was so tired every night that I fell asleep almost instantly, a sense of uneasiness persisted.

It is difficult to describe, even more difficult to explain. There was no repetition of the waking cold of that first night, but every now and then I had the sense of a presence on board. It was so strong at times that when I came back from telephoning or collecting parts or stores I would find myself looking about me as though expecting somebody to be waiting for me.

There was so much to do, and so little time, that I never got around to making determined enquiries as to whether the previous owner had been on that ill-fated voyage. I did write to his address in Kingston, but with no reply I was left with a sense of mystery and the feeling that whatever it was that had happened, it had become imprinted on the fabric of the boat. How else to explain the sense of somebody, something, trying to communicate?

It was August when I bought her, late September when I sailed out of Kinlochbervie bound for Shetland. It would have been more sensible to have headed south to an

English yard, for my deadline to catch the trades across the Atlantic was December. But Scalloway was cheaper. And nearer.

I left with a good forecast, and by nightfall I was motoring north in a flat calm with Cape Wrath light bearing 205° and beginning to dip below the dark line of the horizon. My plan to install larger batteries, an alternator and an automatic pilot had had to be shelved. The money for that was now earmarked for new planking. I stayed on deck, dozing at the helm and watching for trawlers. I was tired before I started and I was tireder now.

A hand touched my shoulder and I woke with a start to complete silence. It was pitch dark, clammily cold. For a moment I couldn't think where I was. Then I saw the shadowy outline of the mainsail above my head. Nothing else—no navigation lights, no compass light, the engine stopped and the boat sluggish. I switched on my torch and the beam shone white on fog. The sails, barely visible, were drawing and we were moving slowly westward, out into the Atlantic.

I pressed the self-starter, but nothing happened, and when I put the wheel over she took a long time to come back on course. I went below then and stepped into a foot or more of water. Fortunately I had installed a powerful, double-action pump. Even so, it took me the better part of four hours to get the water level below the cabin sole. By then it was daylight and the fog had cleared away to the west, a long bank of it looking like a smudge of smoke as the sun glimmered through the damp air.

I tried swinging the engine, but it was no good. Just as well perhaps, because it must have been the prolonged running of the engine that had caused her to take in so much water. Without it the leaks in the planking seemed no worse than when she had been at anchor. I cooked myself a big breakfast on the paraffin stove and it was only when I was sitting over coffee and a cigarette that I remembered how I had woken to the feel of a hand on my shoulder.

I put it out of my mind, not wanting to know about it, and switched to consideration

"See to it! I will not have favourites aboard my ship."

of whether to go on or turn back. But I was already nearly halfway to Shetland and the wind settled the matter by coming from the south-west. I eased sheets and for the next hour we were sailing at almost 6 knots.

The wind held steady all day at Force 3-4, and though there were occasional fog patches I did manage to catch a glimpse of Orkney away to the south-east. Sail trimming and pumping took most of my time, but in the afternoon, when the pump at last sucked dry, I was able to give some thought to navigation.

The tides run strong in the waters between Orkney and Shetland, up to 10 knots in the vicinity of the major headlands, and I had an uneasy feeling I was being carried too far to the east. Just before midnight I sighted what looked like the loom of a light almost over the bows, but my eyes were too tired to focus clearly. I pumped until the bilges sucked dry again, checked the compass and the log, then fell into the quarter berth, still with my oilskins on, not caring whether it was a light or a ship, or whether the boat held her course or not.

I was utterly exhausted and I came out of a dead sleep to see the shadowy figure of a man standing over me. He had something in his hand, and as his arm came up, I rolled off the bunk, hit the floorboards and came up crouched, the hair on my neck prickling, my body trembling.

Maybe I dreamed it; there was nothing there, and the only sound on board the slatting of the sails. But still my body trembled and I was cold with fright. I had a slug of whisky and went up on deck to find the log line hanging inhert, the ship drifting in circles; no wind and the fog like a wet shroud.

I stayed on deck until it got light—a ghostly, damp morning, everything dripping. I pumped the bilges dry, cooked breakfast, attended to the navigation. But though I was fully occupied, I couldn't get it out of my head that I wasn't alone on the ship. Now, whatever I was doing, wherever I was on the boat, I was conscious of his presence.

I know I was tired. But why had my reflexes been so instantaneous? How had I known in the instant of waking that the man standing over me was bent on murder?

The day dragged, the wind coming and going, my world enclosed in walls of fog.

"It's not the best beach for surfing, but now and again we get a wave."

"I dread to think what the hotel will be like."

The circle of sea in which I was imprisoned was never still, enlarging and contracting with the varying density of the fog, and it was cold. Hot tea, exercise, whisky—nothing seemed to dispel that cold. It was deep inside me, a brooding fear.

But of what?

Shetland was getting close now. I knew it would be a tricky landfall, in fog and without an engine. The tidal stream, building up against the long southern finger of the islands, causes one of the worst races in the British Isles. Roost is the local name and the Admiralty Pilot warned particularly of the roost off Sumburgh Head. It would only require a small error of navigation . . . And then, dozing at the helm, I thought I saw two figures in the bows.

I jerked awake, my vision blurred with moisture, seeing them vaguely. But when I rubbed my eyes they were gone. And just before dusk, when I was at the mainmast checking the halyards, I could have sworn there was somebody standing behind me. The fog, tiredness, hallucinations—it is easy not to rationalise. But the ever-present feeling that I was not alone on the boat, the sense of fear, of something terrible hanging over me—that's not so easy to explain.

Night fell, the breeze died and the damp blanket of fog clamped down. I could feel the wetness of it on my eyeballs, my oilskins clammy with moisture and water dripping off the boom as though it were raining. I pumped the bilges dry and had some food. When I came up on deck again there was the glimmer of a moon low down, the boat's head swinging slowly in an eddy. And then I heard it, to the north of me, the soft mournful note of a diaphone—the fog signal on Sumburgh Head.

The tide had just started its main south-easterly flow and within an hour the roost was running and I was in it. The sea became lumpy, full of unpredictable hollows. Sudden overfalls reared up and broke against the top-sides. The movement grew and became indescribable, exhausting, and above the noise of water breaking, the sound of the sails slatting back and forth.

I was afraid of the mast then. I had full main and genoa up. I don't know how long it took me to get the headsail down and lashed, the boat like a mad thing intent on pitching me overboard. An hour maybe. And then the main. I couldn't lash it properly, the movement of the boom too violent. Blood was dripping from a gash in my head where I had been thrown against a winch, my body a mass of bruises. I left the mainsail heaped on deck and wedged myself into the quarter berth. It was the only safe place, the saloon a shambles of crockery and stores, locker doors swinging, the contents flying.

I was scared. The movement was so violent I couldn't pump. I couldn't do anything. I must have passed out from sheer exhaustion when I suddenly saw again the figure standing over the quarter berth, and the thing in his hand was a winch handle. I was seeing it vaguely now, as though from a long way away. I saw the man's arm come up. The metal of the winch handle gleamed. I saw him strike, and as he struck the figure in the bunk moved, rolling out on to the floorboards and coming up in a crouch, his head gashed and blood streaming. There was fear there. I can remember fear then as something solid, a sensation so all-pervading it was utterly crushing, and then the winch handle coming up again and the victim's hand reaching out to the galley where a knife lay, the fingers grasping for it.

I opened my eyes and a star streaked across the swaying hatch. I was on the floor, in a litter of galley equipment, and I had a knife in my hand. As I held it up, staring at it, dazed, the star streaked back across the hatch, the bottom of the mizzen sail showing suddenly white. The significance of that took a moment to sink in, so appalled was I by my experience. The star came and went again, the sail momentarily illuminated; then I was on my feet, clawing my way into the cockpit.

The sky was clear, studded with stars, and to the north the beam of Sumburgh Light swung clear. The fog had gone. There was a breeze from the east now. Somehow I managed to get the genoa hoisted, and inside of half an hour I was sailing in quiet waters clear of the roost.

I went below then and started clearing up the mess. The quarter berth was a tumbled pile of books from the shelf above, and as I was putting them back, a photograph fell to the floor. It showed a man and a woman and two children grouped round the wheel. The man was about 45, fair-haired with a fat, jolly face, his eyes squinting against bright sunlight. I have that picture still, my only contact with the man who had owned *Samoa* before me, the man whose ghostly presence haunted the ship.

By nightfall I was in Scalloway, tied up alongside a trawler at the pier. I didn't sell the boat. I couldn't afford to. And I didn't talk about it. Now that I had seen his picture, knew what he looked like, it seemed somehow less disturbing. I made up my mind I would have to live with it, whatever it was.

I never again used the quarter berth—in fact, I ripped it out of her before I left Scalloway. Sailing south I thought a lot about him in the long night watches. But though I speculated on what must have happened, and sometimes felt he was with me, I was never again identified with him.

Maybe I was never quite so tired again. But something I have to add. From the Azores I headed for Jamaica, and as soon as I arrived in Kingston the boat was the focus of considerable interest. She had apparently been stolen. At least, she had disappeared, and her owner with her. Hi-jacked was the word his solicitors used, for a merchant seaman named O'Sullivan, serving a six-year sentence for armed robbery, had escaped the night before and had never been heard of since. The police now believe he had boarded the boat, hi-jacked her and her owner and sailed her across the Atlantic, probably with Ireland as his objective.

I didn't attempt to see his wife. My experience—what I thought I now knew—could only add to her grief. I sailed at once for the Canal. But though I have tried to put it out of my mind, there are times when I feel his presence lingering. Maybe writing this will help. Maybe it will exorcise his poor, frightened ghost from my mind—or from the boat—whichever it is.

SEVEN CASTAWAY ARTISTS

"The irony of it is that today I should be with Roy Plomley on 'Desert Island Discs.'"

"Lawton, Finney, Matthews, Carter . . . they'll all be retired now, of course."

“*Dear Gert: This is your Tony. Well I have gone straight as you have wanted me to.*”

“*This isn’t the way I imagined it.*”

"The mainland and step on it!"

"I hate to leave him—he was developing into a useful leg-spinner."

Memoirs of an Anglo-Saxon Gondolier

by ALAN COREN

VERY few people know—since the majority of essayists aren't this hard up for opening paragraphs—that the Shorter Oxford Dictionary has chosen p. 1621 to serve up a *double entendre* that would have left Max Miller gasping at the post. For those of you insensitive enough to have left this indispensible vol. to crutch your crippled Steinway, I take my text from the entry: PUNT. "From the L. *ponto*," murmurs the SOD, "a kind of Gallic transport."

A kind of Gallic transport! Could anything be more apt than this vision of a supine, joyous Bardot, breathing gratitude among the embroidered cushions as vernal sunlight dapples her embonpoint, and coupling toads plash in a lusty sub-plot on the bank, acknowledging the Spring with every hormone in their little bodies? Could any *jeu de mots* so suit the wicked punt, that waterborne casting-couch, that mobile boudoir which might have been designed to give the lie to foreign myths of English frigidity? Indeed, it may *only* be in punts that the Anglo-Saxon does achieve anything like Gallic transports: not for us the scented bedchambers hung with Fragonards, not for us the tinkling Geisha house, not for us the motel mating of the Americans, neons winking on the grappling limbs, or the cherooted ladies of the Reperbahn. For the nation whose whole heritage is founded on marine wizardry, whose literature is coursed through and through with the metaphor of rill and weir, whose pond life is the envy of microbiologists throughout the civilised world, what more fitting locale for slap-and-tickle than an honest English punt, creaking among the shallows of an April stream?

Not that this seminal niche of the flat-bottomed boat is its sole position in our history and culture; beyond mere services to lust and love, the punt has given much to England. Search autobiography as you will, you'll find no other single item has played so large a part in the early development of the men who prefixed Great to Britain: remember those grainy shots of Bertrand Russell poling down the Cherwell? Of Winston Churchill painting from his seat among the reeds? Of Lytton Strachey, Edwards VII and VIII, Earl Haig, Lord Alfred Douglas, Hore-Belisha and the young Mountbatten? What else have Algernon Charles Swinburne and Harold Macmillan in common, except that both have coasted down the surface of the Thames without their socks and collars?

Et in Arcadia ego, if you can do that without getting buried first; I too have scattered the minnows on the Isis, eaten cold bangers beneath a rising moon, while unseen midges whanged against my ears and things plopped fishily off either gunwale; I too have stood in a sunken punt, up to my waist among the bobbing bras and bottles, while boy sopranos crooned on Magdalen Tower; I too have lain, willow-hidden, in some Oxford afternoon, arguing the finer metaphysical points of virginity with overdressed young ladies from St. Anne's. The waters of my parking spots have long since cvaporated, the boats themselves have no doubt fallen prey to warp and rot, the girls are all in Surbiton or Hull, married to aging young executives and papering

"*What I like about him, he always shows willing.*"

their walls with Katharine Whitehorn articles; yet somewhere in Time Past, we share a common, unimportant slot.

And sleeping dogs are, after all, only sleeping.

So, therefore:

"Why don't we go punting?" I said.

She turned the hot tap with a dextrous toe.

"You'll fall in," she said. "That's why."

I gave a sardonic chuckle, no easy feat with a toothbrush wedged against one's gum, and the Colgate burgeoning on one's lip like rabies.

"Ten years ago," I said (how lightly falls a decade, eight casual letters!), "no defter forearm wielded pole. My name was a household wo——"

"In Venice," she said, sponging, "you refused to take a gondola on the grounds that it didn't appear in the small print on your policy."

"If you mean," I said, "that I refused to entrust my life to some mandoline-plucker with his mind full of distractions concerning Bostonian widows, you're dead right. There's all the difference in the world between a gigolo in a knotted shirt and crinkly wig and a skilled British pole-artist, a man who's shot Marlowe Bridge in the teeth of a Force Ten——"

My wife yawned eagerly.

"What should I wear?" she said.

"Have you got anything in voile? Or do I mean tulle? And a cartwheel straw hat with cherries on it. Perhaps a parasol, and just a soupcon of——"

"I bet you play a mean ukelele," she said. "Tell me, had the veleta hit Oxford by 1960?"

"I could be getting mixed up with Anna Neagle," I said.

"The wife is always the last to hear," she said.

We got to Oxford just before noon, with the countryside in pregnant bud and the Spring sun mopping up the mist, and every lay-by a dazzling display of station-wagons and children being sick. Over Magdalen Bridge, jostling a gay and colourful throng as old as the motor industry itself, up the beloved curve of the High, and into Cornmarket, which has remained virtually unchanged since the time of Woolworth's. We drove past my old college, which for some reason was playing host to groups of strolling children; my wife claimed they were undergraduates, but I drew a short laugh out of stock and dismissed this uninformed rubbish. Students are far older; I remembered clearly.

We pulled up at last at my favourite punt-station, just behind a North Oxford pub limned in my every dream: beyond its lawns, the river winked, the boatman waited. I dropped the hamper, took his gnarled old hand in mine.

"Tom!" I cried.

"Jim."

"Jim! Of course! It's been a long time, Jim."

He honked something from the back of his throat.

"What has?"

"Show him your forearms," she said. "That'll jog his memory."

My old retainer handed her into the punt, leering.

"Punted before, have you?" he said, shoving the pole lovingly at me.

"Jim!" I cried, "You remember *me*? I always had an Aer Lingus bag with a copy

"I think Henderson is crazed by thirst."

"Do you mind, mate? This lad's swimming the channel."

of *Beowulf* in it, and *The Catcher in the Rye*, and a bottle of Moroccan claret, and a genuine Mexican poncho. I was the first man on the river to have an aerosol gnat-spray."

"You wasn't the tall Welsh bloke with ginger hair, was you?" said Jim, winking furiously at my wife.

"That's him," she said. "He used to come down here with Jessie Matthews."

The boatman wheezed and slapped his skinny thigh, and pushed us off with malevolent vigour. I swayed slightly on the swinging stern, while the pole wriggled curiously in my grasp, alive.

"He's a great kidder, Jim," I explained, thrusting us expertly into the bank.

"And loyal," she said, lurching. "Were you his favourite?"

I shoved off again. And, gradually, the hands rediscovered their cunning, the sensitivity to mud and eddy returned; I might have been a wainwright, dragged by urban desire to some Basingstoke instrument factory, and coming, after ten long years, upon a stricken wain on some incongruous by-pass and dazzling the crowds by bending in his pinstripe suit to cure it with the old, half-hidden skills. I found that swinging, piston rhythm, that fine feel of the wet pole running smoothly through the palms, that delicate flick that holds the punt upon its arrowed course.

"Not bad," she said, trailing a white hand in the olive stream.

"Quite," I said, disguising a breath that came more heavily that I remembered. There is a fine relationship between a man and a girl on a punt, she lying back among the cushions, temporarily passive, he upright, dominant, steering; separated by their roles, they are all innocence; together by the boat, they are inextricably involved, surrounded by a flow that got along quite well for eons without its Freudian annotations.

"There," I said, pointing, "I sat reading poetry to my first girl-friend. Her shins were covered in fine blonde hair."

"Just think," she said, "they may be grey by now."

So I stopped the calling-up of ancient trysts, and rightly so. And, in the warmth of the early afternoon, we parked, and uncorked bottles, and unwrapped quarters of cold duck, and listened to the water slopping softly underpunt. Spring and calm and booze coccooned us, and we lay back among the cushions, smoking, while the birds went about their appointed seductions in the trees above, and far cows lowed.

"You don't happen to remember any poetry, do you?" she murmured.

"I thought you'd never ask," I said.

"So a final dividend of 23% brought the total payments up to 35% on capital, increased by a one-for-ten scrip issue."

"There goes another broken home."

Flotsam

by WAITE

"Never carries a photograph of me."

"Chap on the left is fibreglass—other bloke plywood."

"*You're too late, she's gone.*"

"*I still say we should have bought 'Joyful.'*"

"*I still say we should have bought 'Julia.'*"

How Miles Kington went to Cowes and Changed his Image

PUNCH Central Office is where they look after our image. Mostly it's just little things, like "Coren, get your hair cut" or "Put that secretary down", but once in a while it's a big job. I knew it was a big job last week when I was called to Central Office and the editor offered me some floor near his desk. I stood gratefully.

"We're going to have to re-think you, Kington," he said.

I could see he was angry about something. The little muscle was throbbing behind his left ear, which tells you when he is awake.

"I like myself as I am," I said huskily, flexing my sleeves and lighting a match. I looked hurriedly for my cigarettes.

Patiently, he ignored me.

"If you remember," he said, "we at Central Office started you bicycling just about the same time the Tories got Heath in his first boat. Now, he's Prime Minister, he's winning big races and his image is set fair. What's happened to your bicycling?"

"Had a good run this morning," I said. "Following wind till Knightsbridge, caught the flood tide at Hyde Park Corner, then a zippy port tack down Constitution Hill."

"I'll tell you what's happened. Your trousers have got oil-stains and you bore us all with your interminable biking yarns. Image-wise, nothing."

"I'm not sure I reckon these newfangled Moultons," I said. "Oh, they're all right with a following wind and good visibility, but what use are those small wheels in squall and deep puddles? Give me a heavy old Humber any day, with an easterly headwind coming down the Mall and the rainclouds storming in across Nelson's shoulders."

"Tomorrow's your big chance, Kington. Heath can't go to Cowes for his race. But you can. We know a man who's got a boat. Tomorrow you become a sailor."

He turned away and wrote a quick article to signify the interview was over. Stunned, I wandered down the corridor and bumped into Coren.

"You keep your oily turn-ups to yourself," he snarled.

"I'm going racing at Cowes tomorrow," I said dully. "Any urgent messages can be left at the Island Sailing Club."

He goggled slightly and a new respect flickered across his face. By God, it's true, I thought; the image is improved already.

Minutes later I was speeding effortlessly by train, taxi and hovercraft to Cowes where I spent a fascinating few hours locating the Island Club. The streets were thronged with wind-burnt men in blue clothes, strong and silent like grizzled waiters

"If this power crisis comes, Mildred, we're going to have to learn to sail."

and none of them speaking English. Eventually I stopped an Australian sailor who explained to me with copious sign language that I was standing in, if not blocking, the entrance to the Club. It was there I met my two fellow crew members, Roy and Peter. They didn't speak English either.

"Halyard?" I said, "Starboard jib sheet? Fo'c'sle? L'ndl'bb'r? Qu'est-ce que c'est que tout ca?"

"Sorry, old boy," said Roy. "Quite forgot you didn't understand. We'll tell you all about it before John turns up in the morning. He's the skipper, but he's at the Squadron Ball tonight."

After egg and sausage next morning he took me on a tour of the boat and explained in child's language how to hoist sails, get spinnaker booms up, control the jib, operate the topping-lift and meet Sir Max Aitken. By the end of it I felt that even if I still didn't know the ropes, I knew they weren't called ropes but sheets. Then John arrived, fresh from a few minutes sleep after the Ball, and reported on the great occasion. I didn't understand all the jargon, but it seemed that there had been a slight collision during the second waltz and a formal protest had been lodged.

We arrived shortly after ten in the main arena where the various races were due to start from, in the midst of a huge fleet of boats ranging from small dinghies to huge Admiral's Cup craft with trained teams of gymnasts arranged photogenically from fore to aft. Guns fired. Boats dashed off. Stopwatches were set. John had a beer. Roy stared through the binoculars.

"They've given us course 55," he reported.

"That's a long one—right down the Solent and into the sea," said John.

"I've arranged to meet my wife at 6.30," said Peter, apropos of nothing.

"You handle the winching handle on the jib winch, Miles," said Roy.

I said nothing.

"We're a bit over the line. We'll have to go back," said Roy.

"Prepare to go about," said John. I looked expectant. "Right, go about!"

The boat turned, sheets whistled, sails flapped.

"Wunchargdle!" yelled Roy. I looked interested. "WUNCHARGDLE!" He pulled out the winching handle and thrust it at me. I tightened the winch and suddenly, from feeling small, I felt good.

"Correction," said Roy. "We weren't over the line at all."

Curses. Going about again. Swearing and depression, except for me who had got the winching handle in without prompting. Our starting gun fired and we headed for the distant starting line.

With all respect to Punch Central Office, as well as Mr. Heath, I think it's best to be the most junior on a boat. Let others argue the merits of various courses—catch a bit

"About this sea-serpent . . ."

"I think I know why we keep travelling in circles."

of wind here, avoid a bad tide there—and sit back in the cockpit, watching the sun come out slowly in complete defiance of the forecast and clutching the wunchargdle just in case.

"Put away that damned handle," said Roy.

Most of the boats in our class were ahead of us. We expected this, as ours was low in the classification and therefore had a good handicap. In fact there were only six boats reckoned to be slower, and there were six or more behind us. A good race. The boat level with us was called Braganza.

"Supposed to be faster, too," said Roy, consulting the library. "But they're not pointing as well as us." I looked a silent question. "They can't keep as close to the wind—they'll have to tack across before the next mark, then we'll be ahead. Got a job for you now, Miles."

I reached for the wunchargdle.

"You can make some lunch."

Down in the galley I made some s'rd'ne s'nd'ches. This done is by sliding the key in the loop and winching across the top of the tin, then unballasting the s'rd'nes on to packed bread while falling from one side of the galley to the other. Hours later I emerged.

"See that small black dot over there?" said Roy.

"No," I said.

"That's Braganza."

I went below again to wash lettuce. When I reappeared there was a boat just ahead. It was Braganza. John was issuing instructions for hoisting the spinnaker as soon as we rounded Bembridge Lodge. We went about, the jib came down but the spinnaker didn't go up. John cursed his crew for a pack of scurvy knaves. We smiled and sweated. The spinnaker went up but we had lost ground. Only four boats behind us now.

By four o'clock we were in front of Cowes again and heading past on the last leg. We had spent a leisurely afternoon thankfully packing the spinnaker away, watching Braganza pointedly badly and getting wet as the forecast started coming true. It was then we realised that there were no boats behind us.

"They've all packed up and gone home," said Roy. "It's only us and Braganza now."

Braganza chose this moment to slide gracefully astern towards Cowes, waving.

"It's only us now," said Roy.

"Never mind," said John, "we'll have another go with the spinnaker on the homeward run."

There was silence.

"Said I'd meet my wife at 6.30," said Peter absently.

"Class I's having trouble with their spinnakers," said Roy vaguely.

"Madam, would you mind removing your hat?"

"That's settled, then—we won't handle containers."

"I sense that we have an anti-spinnaker faction on board," said John sternly. "You win."

"Belay there," I cried, leaping into Punch Central Office and spitting on the carpet. The editor looked up at my wind-swept features.

"Brush your hair," he muttered.

"Oh, it's you," he said. "Did you win?"

"It's a very complicated system of classification," I said. "But my wife looked at me with a new respect last night when I got back."

"Did you win?" he said sternly.

"Although we came last," I said, "I cannot describe to you the magic of being out in the spray, with the halyards slapping the mast and the creaking of the sheets. I have discovered a new world . . ."

"Last?" said Punch Central Office. "I have a new idea, Kington. Why not give bicycling another try?"

ALAN HACKNEY:

Red Sailors Whiter than White — *Official*

"Debauches of American sailors in Mediterranean ports have become the talk of the town. Their visits result in armed attacks on shops", but Russian sailors ashore make for the museums and "visit places of interest. They are polite to residents and very kind to children". That's what the magazine RED STAR tells us.

"HOW many more bleeding rooms in this gallery, Chief Petty Officer? Half of us are shagged out already. Etruscan, Roman, medieval, I dunno."

"Pack that moaning in, Leading Seaman Petrov, put your cap on straight and let's have a bit more interested smiling at the ceramics."

"What times does this place close, Chief? Only my boots are killing me. I mean, yesterday we done four solid hours round that Town Hall."

"Pipe down, Stoker Prokoviev. Stop behaving like an imperialist."

"You know, Petrov, what it is, we never should have joined."

"You're bloody right, Prokoviev. There was never no talk of this horrible bloody image caper when we went round the recruiting centre. All that gaff about having a look round the decadent permissive western ports. All that winking and nudging. I mean, I know they never actually *said*, but still."

"Tell you what, Petrov, hang back a bit. Then when the Chief gets the rest of the party round the corner to the mummies we can . . ."

"Stoker Prokoviev!"

"Yes, Chief?"

"See that local resident there, twenty yards to starboard? Nip across smartish and kiss her baby."

"Her what? What, me, Chief?"

"Yes you, Prokoviev. Let's have a great big smile and then smartly back at the double and no chatting-up. Clear? Away you go, then."

"Chief, when Stoker Prokoviev's done his bit over there in the line of duty and that, how about us knocking off for a bit and nip over the bar across the road outside? Promise not to talk to any girls. All right?"

"What do you think you're on, lad, an orgy? Culture's what this day ashore's about. Culture and friendship with the locals.

"I thought perhaps just a couple of vodkas, Chief."
"Petrov's right, Chief. It's dead thirsty work traipsing round all these statues and pictures. Anyway, it must be bad for our wossname—Marxist-Leninist doctrinal purity."
"Don't try coming the old acid with me, lad. Right, our next port of call's room fourteen, Renaissance Tapestries. Ah, Stoker Prokoviev, made your contact, did you?"
"I wasn't the only one, Chief. That kid took a nip out of my finger. Got fangs like a bleeding wolf."
"Never mind, lad. The local female resident make any comment, did she?"
"Offered to take me round to the local hospital."
"Ah, but you told her we had excellent medical facilities on Soviet ships?"
"No, I told her if I didn't report back to you right away you'd make a necktie of my—."
"That's enough of that, Prokoviev. Get fell in. Right, follow me."
"What was the bird like, Prokoviev?"
"Lovely. Legs right up to her waist and giving off a touch of Arpège."
"Game, do you reckon?"
"Never had a chance to find out, did I? I was just going to ask her round behind them display cabinets when the chico sunk his choppers into me."
"Hard luck, mate. Still, that's as near as any of us are likely to get to the local crumpet on this culture lark."
"Stroll on! What's on the cards for tomorrow, then?"
"Catacombs, followed by a lunchtime concert with some old ladies."
"Here, Petrov, you reckon we could lose the Chief down the catacombs then swear blind we went to the concert? He wouldn't dare report he'd lost us. I reckon if most

of us couldn't manage to have it away during the siesta we're a disgrace to Mother Russia."

"Definitely. Right, you're on."

"Stoker Prokoviev! You men! Come along here, stop hanging about. Take a look at this Tiepolo ceiling. Done by this Italian, it was, seventeenth century or thereabouts, probably for some Pope. Total number of human and mystical figures, three hundred and sixty five, all arranged in and about this pattern of cloud formations. Get your notebooks open and let's see those pencils moving . . ."

"Here, Chief, look. Over there. There's a party of Yank sailors come in and going around!"

"What? Where? Ah, trying to get in on the act, I don't doubt. Right, close ranks, lads, keep your eyes on the ceiling above. Ignore them. Don't worry, we've got a head start. They'll never look convincing in a million years."

"They don't seem to be enjoying it much, Chief."

"Exactly, lad. The American imperialists are lacking in any natural culture or sense of duty, serving only the twin gods of pleasure and profit. Any questions about this ceiling so far?"

"Hey, Prokoviev, some of those Yanks look pissed as newts."

"Lucky bastards. I bet they took some getting out of the night clubs to be dragged round here."

"D'you think their Admiral's been reading Red Star as well as ours? They don't want to believe what they read in the bloody papers."

"Right, everybody over by those nuns and what appear to be orphans. Leading Seaman Petrov, off cap and place it on one of their heads. Stoker Prokoviev, get your Leningrad out, we'll have a photo. Everybody look up at the ceiling and point! Smile, comrades, or I'll have you chasing round a couple of amphitheatres before we get back aboard. Hold it. Lovely. Okay, Yankees, try and follow that!"

"*What a waste, Harry, that this should happen to a man with your contacts.*"

"Bingo!"

"Have you got any caviar?"